WISDOM COMMENTARY SERIES

JONAH

Wisdom Commentary Series: Jonah

Author: Stephen Davey

Editor: Jarl K. Waggoner

Cover Design & Body Layout: Kristin C. Preston

Photo of Stephen: Sam Gray Portraits, Raleigh, NC (samgrayportraits.com)

ISBN 978-1-944189-20-4

Published by Charity House Publishers

Charity House Publishers, Inc.

2703 Jones Franklin Road

Suite 105

Cary, North Carolina 27518

USA

www.wisdomonline.org

To the memory of my friend and mentor
~ *Wendell Kempton* ~
who for forty years refused to alter or reverse his course
in passionately reaching the lost for Christ and
whose legacy continues to impact and encourage me
to serve our Lord with perseverance and
— no matter what —
stay the course!

CONTENTS

The word of the Lord came to Jonah the son of Amittai

–Jonah 1:1

CHAPTER ONE

MORE THAN A FISH STORY

Jonah 1:1

M ention Zaccheus to most Christians, and they'll think of a short guy who climbed a sycamore tree; bring up Daniel, and most people recall a lion's den; drop Noah's name, and the ark soon follows. Start a conversation about Jonah, and most people will immediately think of a man who was swallowed by a whale.

We all tend to remember the sensational elements of biblical accounts. But there is a lot more to Noah than an ark; there is a lot more to Daniel than the lions' den and to Zaccheus than climbing a tree; and there is certainly much more to Jonah than a whale.

The book of Jonah is most often considered little more than an interesting fish story. It is more than that. In less than fifty verses of scripture, we observe a storm at sea, the conversion of idolatrous sailors, a miraculous rescue, a song of praise, the repentance of a brutal nation, and the unfolding revelation of God's relationship to unrepentant Gentiles, not to mention a very disobedient prophet. Furthermore, we see God work through His creation—the wind, a fish, a vine, and a worm. In many ways Jonah is a microcosm of God's relationship with and sovereignty over all creation, all kingdoms, and all history.[1]

The trouble is we fail to connect Jonah and the *greatest* national revival ever recorded—following the *shortest* sermon ever preached! We rarely con-

nect Jonah to the mercy of God. We forget that Jonah was the first mission-
ary in human history sent by God to a Gentile nation. In fact, we never
think about Jonah being the only prophet on record sent to a heathen nation
with a message of repentance.[2] Worse yet, we don't immediately think of
Jonah as the signature sign of the resurrection of Jesus Christ.

Indeed, the book of Jonah is much more than a fish story.

OBJECTIONS TO THE STORY OF JONAH

It is little wonder Satan has attempted throughout history to make
the book of Jonah the butt of jokes, smears, and sneers. For centuries, liberal professors and pastors, along with many other so-called scholars, have
attempted to downplay, discredit, deconstruct, and thus destroy the credibility of these forty-eight inspired verses of Scripture. Their disbelief follows
along the lines of five primary objections.

1. First, they object to the abundance of miracles.

Frankly, we would expect this. They do not believe God sent a fish to
swallow Jonah. In fact, they do not believe God created fish to begin with, so
why should we expect them to believe God could command a fish to swallow
a man? They do not believe God created the plants and animals in Genesis
1, so why would we expect them to believe Jonah 1?

We will never convince an unbeliever of God's unlimited power until
that person places his or her faith in the power of God's Son. Until then, the
unsaved person, Paul wrote, "does not receive the things of the Spirit of God,
for they are spiritually discerned" (1 Corinthians 2:14).

2. Second, they consider Jonah a fairy tale because of the rather unique mission of Jonah.

Liberal scholars point out that God had never before commissioned a
Jewish prophet to go to a Gentile nation. Therefore, this obviously must
be a story spun to make the Jewish people feel superior. Is God confined
to acting like most church congregations—doing only what has been done
before and never anything different? Just because He had never before sent
a prophet to a Gentile nation does not mean He *would* not. Indeed, under
God's direction, both Elijah and Elisha made contact with pagan kings, so

for Jonah to be commissioned as a special envoy to a pagan people is not difficult to imagine.

3. **Third, liberals object to this story because Jonah refers to Nineveh in the past tense.**

In chapter 3 Jonah writes, **Now Nineveh was an exceedingly great city.** The argument is that the past tense indicates Nineveh was no longer in existence at the time the book of Jonah was written, indicating it was composed at a much later date and by someone other than the prophet. However, the use of *was* is perfectly acceptable in narrative writing. And most of the book of Jonah is just that—narrative.

4. **A fourth objection is that Jonah could never have been in Nineveh at all because he states that it took three days to walk through the city when we know Nineveh was small enough to travel through in a single day.**

Oh? What about the outlying areas? What about the suburbs of this leading city of Assyria, a kingdom that overpowered the northern kingdom of Israel?

We know its population was larger than the current population of Charleston, South Carolina, Boulder, Colorado, or my home city of Cary, North Carolina. If we tried to deliver a message of coming doom to the

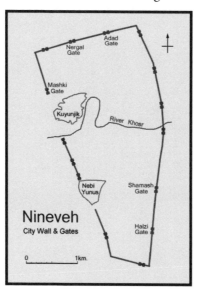

more than 130,000 people living in my hometown, traveling on foot from one end of Cary to the other, it would easily take several days—if not weeks.

How the unbelieving world grasps at straws.

5. A final objection is that Jonah uses some words that seem incompatible with his vocabulary.

Aren't we glad these scholars know Jonah's vocabulary so well? The truth is that the words in question appear in Old Testament books both before Jonah's time and after.[3] And I would venture a guess that Jonah had read the Old Testament Scriptures at some point in his devotions.

The truth remains: Jonah is not make-believe. He was a real man, living in a real time, with a real challenge on his hands.

BACKGROUND OF JONAH

Jonah, in fact, had already been around quite a while before he wrote his book. He was the court prophet for Jeroboam II, who reigned in the northern kingdom of Israel 750 years before the birth of Christ.

Jonah had already delivered a rather famous prophecy that had been fulfilled when the northern kingdom regained some of its lost territory.

> [Jeroboam] restored the border of Israel from the entrance of
> Hamath as far as the Sea of the Arabah, according to the word
> of the Lord, the God of Israel, which He spoke through His
> servant Jonah, the son of Amittai. (2 Kings 14:25)

This verse corroborates the time and place of Jonah's ministry. Second Kings even mentions Jonah's hometown, which was in the region that became known during the days of Christ as Galilee.

Imagine that. The prophet whose biography would provide an illustration of Christ's resurrection was prophesying in the same neighborhood where Jesus Christ would later live and preach.

Jonah was among the leading prophets of his generation. His contemporaries were Hosea and Amos. In fact, it is very likely Jonah had been trained by his predecessor, Elisha.[4] J. Sidlow Baxter wrote, "Jonah would have been a leading prophet among the schools of the prophets when Elisha was nearing the end of his remarkable ministry."[5]

Like Elisha, Jonah was among the revered prophets of the Jewish people. More than likely, the father of the apostles Peter and Andrew was named after Jonah. Peter was known originally as *Simon barjona* (Matthew 16:17). *Bar* means *son of.* Simon, therefore, was the son of a man named Jonah—perhaps in honor of the famous prophet of Israel.[6]

To the average Jewish person of Jesus' time, Jonah was the prophet of old who had helped Israel succeed. He had preached the greatest evangelistic campaign in Israel's history, seeing the pagan people of Nineveh come to faith in God.

Josephus, the first-century Jewish historian, included Jonah in his *Antiquities of the Jews.* He wrote, "But since I have promised to give an exact account of our history, I have thought it necessary to recount what I have found written in the Hebrew books concerning this prophet [Jonah]."[7]

Jonah is neither fantasy nor fiction. He was for real.

INTRODUCTION TO JONAH

Jonah's account actually opens with the Hebrew waw, a prefix that is appropriately translated "and," though it is left untranslated in many Bible versions. This opening construction reveals the interesting point that verse 1 of Jonah seems to be continuing something that immediately preceded it. However, we are not told what that is.

Warren Wiersbe noted that if one of his books began with the word *and,* the editor would probably wonder if something had been lost—including Wiersbe's ability to use the English language. He went on to write that by opening with the word *and,* the book of Jonah hints to us that God's story of grace and mercy is a continuing message.[8]

The word of the Lord came to Jonah. (Jonah 1:1)

Whenever we read the word of the Lord came to [someone], we need to recognize it as a formulaic phrase that marks a true prophet of God.[9] It authenticated the true prophet as opposed to a false one, or it indicated someone other than a prophet was being asked to participate in a special mission of God. For Jonah, it was the authentic mark of his prophetic ministry.[10]

The word of the Lord coming to someone also meant something was about to happen. Someone was about to step into action. *Something* was going to happen to *someone*.

In the meantime, *nothing* is said about Jonah himself. There is nothing about his birthplace or his previous ministry. We have absolutely no introduction.[11] We're not even told how the word of the Lord came to him. Was it through a dream or a vision in the night? Did it come by way of a heavenly voice or an angel? We don't know. There are no details—just the barest of facts.

Perhaps you're already aware that everything in this book seems to happen in fast motion. Absolutely everything that can be left out is. Nothing clutters the landscape of this account.

There is only one introductory comment made about Jonah:

The word of the Lord came to Jonah the son of Amittai.
(Jonah 1:1)

Who is **Amittai?** Again, we don't know, and evidently it is of little importance.

However, the meanings of both these men's names are very interesting and give us a picture of the coming drama. **Jonah** is the Hebrew word for *dove*. Often, children of believing Hebrews would be named after animals in the hope they would grow up to exhibit everything good about the creatures' best characteristics.[12] The dove was known for gentleness, harmlessness, flight, and most significantly, peace.

Ever since Genesis 8:11, when the dove flew back to Noah with an olive branch or leaf in its beak, the dove has been a symbol of hope and peace. In fact, to this day around the world, the phrase, "to extend an olive branch," means to make an offer of peace. In addition, when the dove is seen on flags, emblems, or banners, it is always in flight, signifying its role as a messenger.

Jonah would live out his name. He would be sent as a messenger to extend the olive branch of peace with God to a nation on the brink of judgment. Jonah, the "Dove," would be commissioned by the Emperor of heaven to serve as the ambassador of peace.

Jonah was **the son of Amittai.** Amittai's name comes from the Hebrew root word that means faithful or true and gives us the word *amen*, which is used as an oath or verbal confirmation of truth.

So, **Jonah the son of Amittai** could be paraphrased, "The messenger of peace, the son of truth." This is much more than coincidence. Here is the messenger of peace sent to tell the truth to a pagan people.

Jonah didn't go to the Ninevites to talk to them about peace, love, and joy. He went to tell them the truth: "If you don't repent, you will be destroyed by the holy God." Keep in mind the implied order: No one can have *peace* with God without believing the *truth* of God. Jonah delivered the truth, effectively living out his name.

However, we also remember his reluctance to do so. Let's not be too hard on this "dove," though, until we discover the details.

Jonah was commanded to offer peace to a nation known for merciless brutality. The Assyrians were legendary for dismembering their enemies one limb at a time, leaving only the right arm and hand so they could shake their enemies' hands and smile at them as they watched them die.

In addition, Jonah was not given any assurance that he would be listened to or even survive his mission. We might have been ready to buy a ticket out of town too!

AN OVERVIEW OF JONAH

We can easily outline the book of Jonah biographically with five simple points:

1. See Jonah Run
2. See Jonah Swim
3. See Jonah Fly
4. See Jonah Preach
5. See Jonah Pout

We could also outline the book, as did one commentator, by paralleling Jonah's ministry with the story of the prodigal son (Luke 15). In the first two chapters, Jonah plays the role of the son who runs away from his father. He carries the inheritance of His Father's riches but chooses to keep it for himself.

In the last two chapters, Jonah plays the role of the prodigal's older brother, who pouts and refuses to enter into the joyful homecoming of a repentant brother.[13]

No matter how we outline the book, however, it should be clear that "The Prodigal Prophet" is an appropriate subtitle for Jonah.

KEY LESSONS FROM JONAH

Before we dive in (no pun intended) to this fascinating book, what are some of the key lessons that are immediately observable?

- **First, be alert: God has delivered His word to *us* as well.**

Have you ever thought about the fact that the word of the Lord has come to you, too? It has. You have at least one copy of it nearby—it's called the Bible.

You might be tempted to say, "Yes, but I'm not like Jonah. I'm not a prophet."

I'm not a prophet either, and I am not the son of a prophet. In fact, I even work for a nonprofit! But the truth remains, God has spoken—to you and to me.

> He spoke long ago to the fathers in the prophets in many portions and in many ways, [and] in these last days [He] has spoken to us in His Son. (Hebrews 1:1–2)

We hold in our hands the words of the prophets and the words of Christ and His apostles.

> And it is profitable for teaching, for reproof, for correction, for training in righteousness so that the man of God [the believer] may be adequate, equipped for every good work. (2 Timothy 3:16–17)

God has spoken! Be alert to what God is saying to you through His Word. It will equip you for the journey He leads you on in life.

- **Second, be encouraged: God can use *anyone* and anything to accomplish His will.**

Watch as God uses pagan sailors, a storm at sea, a rather large fish, a plant and a worm, and a stubborn, runaway prophet. This is the grace of God in living color. Even fallen, faltering Jonah was God's choice to bring about a national revival.

- **Third, be careful: past obedience doesn't guarantee *future* obedience.**

I agree with those who believe Jonah was likely an old man when the events in this book occurred.[14] His greatest test was reserved for his later years. This is much like Daniel who was around eighty-five years of age when he was thrown to the lions.

Jonah had served God for decades. He had rubbed shoulders with Elisha, prophesied before kings, and perhaps taught a few courses in the school of the prophets. No one would have been surprised to learn that Jonah was given this incredibly dangerous and difficult commission from God. Jonah was the man!

Frankly, I think Jonah would be somewhat embarrassed to know that three thousand years later, believers like us would be embarking on a close scrutiny of his actions, his emotions, his pride, his fears, and his failures. I think he would be embarrassed to know we are about to pour over every word and explore every corner and crevice of his biography.

And what a shocking revelation—Jonah had years of faithful service as a prophet of God, and we have only *one* verse about it in 2 Kings. But he had a few months of utter failure, and we have an entire book about it.

I am reminded of one of God's purposes in recording all of Israel's failures along their journey. Paul explained, "These accounts were given to you as an example" (1 Corinthians 10:6). In other words, these accounts teach us both what to do and what not to do.

We should be grateful God didn't give us detailed accounts on Jonah's successes and only one verse on his failures. We wouldn't learn nearly enough of what we need in our own struggle with obedience and courage.

Jonah is a book for saints who get it wrong. It is also a book to amaze and thrill and challenge us to get it right. Jonah's years of faithful service in the past did not guarantee faithful service in the future. The same is true of us. None of us have reached the tape quite yet.

So, be alert, be encouraged, but be careful.

²"Arise, go to Nineveh the great city and cry against it, for their wickedness has come up before Me." ³But Jonah rose up to flee to Tarshish from the presence of the Lord. So he went down to Joppa, found a ship which was going to Tarshish, paid the fare and went down into it to go with them to Tarshish from the presence of the Lord.

–Jonah 1:2–3

CHAPTER TWO

SEE JONAH RUN

Jonah 1:2–3

What comes to mind when you think of the dirtiest, crummiest, most difficult job on the planet? Maybe you think you have it!

After a little researching, I discovered jobs almost too difficult to imagine. One of them was sewage inspector. The article provided a photograph of a man dressed in a full body suit, oxygen tanks strapped on his back, a diver's hood pulled and taped securely, and a mask and thick gloves. The photograph showed him waist deep, descending a ladder, eventually to disappear into raw sewage. You might be thinking your college roommate would be perfect for the job.

A little more digging surfaced a list of the ten categories of most dangerous jobs. Number eight on the list was forestry jobs—primarily lumberjacks. Because of hidden roots, high winds, and working with chainsaws a hundred feet in the air, these are among the world's most dangerous jobs.

Further up the list is the category of military, police, and fire personnel. Every day on the job is a risk for these people, as they put their lives on the line.

Steelworkers, roofers, and crane operators form another category high on the list of dangerous professions. Many people die each year while operating heavy machinery or working high above ground.

The number one category for endangered employees is the field of transportation: fishermen, pilots, and bus and truck drivers. Literally hundreds of people die each year as they travel by land, sky, or sea.

If we rolled the clock back to the Old Testament era, we would find that one of the most dangerous jobs on the planet was that of a prophet.

- Elijah had a contract on his head, courtesy of his own queen.

- Jeremiah was beaten, imprisoned several times, and thrown into a well, where he sank to his waist in the mud and was left to die.

- Daniel was thrown to lions.

- Nehemiah was threatened with his life soon after moving to Jerusalem. At one point he and his men worked to restore the city walls of Jerusalem with a trowel in one hand and a sword in the other.

To this day, there might not be anything more difficult or dangerous than obeying the will of God.

Jonah was seasoned, experienced, and dedicated to King Jeroboam and the nation Israel. His prophecy to Jeroboam and the nation had come to pass, adding to Jonah's credibility and fame. He was definitely made of the same mettle as his mentor, Elisha, but when God called him into a new chapter of ministry—the most difficult yet—Jonah chose to run away.

The prophet's years of faithful service to God undoubtedly had taught him the dangers involved in obeying God. He would soon learn that *disobeying* God held its own dangers.

JONAH'S CALL FROM GOD

Listen to the call Jonah received from God.

"Arise, go to Nineveh the great city and cry against it, for their wickedness has come up before Me." (Jonah 1:2)

We could paraphrase that last phrase, "They smell to the highest heavens."[1] In other words, God was saying, "Jonah, Nineveh has become a city of sinful sewage. Their stench has reached heaven. Get on your prophet's gear, tape on your mask, strap on your tanks, and go deliver a message to them: clean it up . . . or else."

The command from God certainly got Jonah's attention. And the destination of his assignment must have immediately overwhelmed him with distasteful emotions—emotions that eventually led him to resign as a prophet of God. If we climb back into Jonah's culture, we will better understand why.

Nineveh was the chief city of Assyria. The Assyrian Kingdom was a constant threat to Israel and would eventually take Israel into captivity. The city of Nineveh was located in modern Iraq, near the northern city of Mosul.[2] The Assyrians would rule this portion of the world until conquered by the Babylonians around 150 years after Jonah's death.

Much of Nineveh has been excavated, and much of the city's walls were reconstructed using original material. The city obviously was once an impressive fortress, built for war by a warring people. They were Israel's most feared enemies.

Jonah would eventually walk through the central gate of Nineveh, which has also been reconstructed on its original site in Iraq, using some of the excavated, original stones.[3] The towers of the gate stood nearly three hundred feet in the air. It was a breathtaking and intimidating introduction to the grandeur of Nineveh and the power of the Assyrian Kingdom. God even refers to it here in verse 2 as **the great city**.

Reconstruction of Nineveh's Nirgal Gate, the city's principal gate

Thanks to the work of archaeologists, we now know much about the palace of the Assyrian king. The palace was beautifully and colorfully painted with battle scenes and warrior gods.

When the king of Assyria assumed the throne, he supposedly joined the hand of deity, which invested in him the power of the national god, Marduk. The vast empire the king ruled would at its peak stretch from the Persian Gulf to the borders of Egypt.[4]

Depiction of the interior of the Nineveh Palace

Above all, the Assyrians were known by the Jews for their occultism, bloodlust, cruelty, and ferocity in battle.

The prophet Nahum would also prophesy against Nineveh with this description:

> Woe to the bloody city, completely full of lies and pillage; her prey never departs, the noise of the whip, the noise of the rattling of the wheel, galloping horses and bounding chariots! Horsemen charging, swords flashing, spears gleaming, many slain, a mass of corpses, and countless dead bodies . . . because of the many harlotries of the harlot, the charming one, the mistress of sorceries, who sells nations by her harlotries and families by her sorceries. "Behold, I am against you," declares the Lord of hosts. (Nahum 3:1–4)

The Ninevites were demon-worshiping, immoral, brutal, unmerciful people. They boasted of their cruelty. Excavated records reveal their armies parading with the heads of their vanquished enemies elevated on poles. They boasted of stretching live prisoners with ropes so they could be more easily skinned alive. One king boasted, "I flayed the skin from as many nobles as had rebelled against me and draped their skin over the pile of corpses. I burned their children. I captured many troops alive and cut off their arms, hands, noses, ears, and extremities."[5]

It was an Assyrian custom to gouge out the eyes of prisoners or put hooks in their noses and humiliate them by leading them like cattle before slaughtering them. They would impale their captives alive (a precursor of crucifixion, which was perfected by the Romans) and then set them on fire. Nero, the Roman emperor, would repeat this practice by impaling Christians, covering them with tar, and setting them on fire to light his garden parties.

Assyrian king putting out the eyes of a captive, who, with others, is held prisoner with hooks in the lips

Even the excavated hinges on the city gates of Nineveh, which Jonah himself would have seen, graphically depicted their cruelty to captives. They were proud of the terror they struck in the hearts of their enemies; they were proud of their reputation for being unmerciful.

It is no wonder that in the end Jonah effectively said to God, "I did not want You to show them mercy" (Jonah 4:2 paraphrased).

Still, God's call and command to Jonah were clear.

- **The command from God didn't allow for any confusion.**

Jonah didn't miss the point. God made His will perfectly clear to His prophet. The verbs, **arise, go,** and **cry against,** or speak out, are not suggestions. In the Hebrew language, these are imperatives, commands that could have exclamation points after them.[6]

When we fail to obey God, it isn't because we don't understand Him, because we *do*. We just don't like it when God uses imperatives. We prefer suggestions. We believe in voting—God has one vote and we do too.

But God isn't in the practice of handing out ballots.

Arise . . . go . . . cry—Jonah didn't have to go into his study, pull out his Hebrew lexicon, and parse these verbs to make sure he understood them.[7] God's commands were unmistakable, undeniable, and entirely *upsetting*.

- **The commission from God didn't attempt to hide reality.**

This was not a sales pitch. God said, **Their wickedness has come up before me.** In other words, "Their perversion and wickedness and cruelty have not gone unnoticed. I know what I'm asking you to do, and I understand how difficult it will be to confront them with the truth."

We are sometimes tempted to think that if God really *knew* what is involved in doing what He has called us to do and the difficulty it creates in our minds and hearts and bodies, He certainly would *never* call us to do it! Such thinking demonstrates not only lack of faith but also woeful ignorance of God and His ways.

This commission was the will of God for Jonah:

- whether he felt good about it or not,
- whether he wanted to do it or not,
- whether he agreed with God or not,
- whether he was uncomfortable or not,
- whether he was fearful or not,
- whether he was happy where he was or not,
- whether he thought the Ninevites were worth it or not.

Jonah had walked with God and spoken for God in pleasant places and to receptive audiences. Now it was time for him to **arise, go to Nineveh— and cry against it.**

The command of God didn't allow for confusion, and it didn't ignore reality.

- **The call of God didn't guarantee safety.**

God's call did not include a single guarantee for Jonah's benefit. God's command wasn't laced with promises of a successful trip and a comfortable return. Jonah was not offered a benefit package for courageous prophets: the assurance of a listening audience; a welcome by the Ninevites; hospitality offered in a cruel environment.

Jonah was simply commanded to announce to a brutal nation that they were all going to die in forty days unless they repented, abandoned Marduk, and followed the God of Israel. Jonah had every reason to believe his head would be attached to a long pole after his first day in Nineveh.

There were no loopholes in Jonah's call and no guarantees of safe conduct and a safe landing back home. Frankly, this was a call from God to do something impossible.

What is God asking you to do for Him that you are resisting? What is His impossible assignment for you? What is it that stops you from taking the first step? Maybe you have an entire grocery-list of fears, excuses, and good reasons why it won't work. Perhaps it is disappointment with past attempts that is holding you back or a lack of assurances that this new step of faith will pay off. Or maybe it's just not what you expected or wanted from God. After all, God's will surely is never upsetting, uncomfortable, unhealthy, or undesirable.

For Jonah, it was all the above. He knew what obeying God meant. And in his mind there was only one thing he could do. There was only one response that made sense to him—run!

JONAH'S RESPONSE

But Jonah rose up to flee to Tarshish from the presence of the Lord. So he went down to Joppa, found a ship which was going to Tarshish, paid the fare and went down into it to go with them to Tarshish from the presence of the Lord. (Jonah 1:3)

See Jonah run!

But don't be too quick to judge. Elijah ran for his life from Queen Jezebel. One woman's threat made the prophet of God run into hiding (1 Kings 19:3). At least Jonah was running from an entire *kingdom*.

To get your bearings on Jonah's flight, keep in mind that Jonah was originally from Gath-hepher and most likely living at the time in Samaria, the capital of the northern kingdom of Israel. During the time Jonah served the Lord, he lived about thirty miles northeast of **Joppa**, a port city on the coast of the Mediterranean Sea. Joppa was Israel's primary port city.

Modern port city of Jaffa, biblical Joppa

Surely Jonah knew he couldn't literally run from the presence of the Lord for God is omnipresent. Yes, Jonah undoubtedly knew David's words well: "Where can I go from Your Spirit? Or where can I flee from Your presence?" (Psalm 139:7). Jonah knew he couldn't outrun God.

The text informs us that Jonah was running away **from the presence of the Lord,** effectively abandoning his role as a prophet. He was *resigning* from serving under—and in partnership with—the power and presence of God.

The New Jewish Version translates this phrase "the service of the Lord," underscoring that Jonah was actually running from the Lord's service as a prophet.[8] Jonah was effectively turning in his resignation. He was quitting.

He was saying to God, "I've had it. I will no longer be a prophet of the Lord." And to prove it, he left Israel for good and set sail for Tarshish.

Tarshish, located on the coast of Spain, was in the exact opposite direction from Nineveh. In fact, Tarshish was considered the most western spot of the known world. Jonah was not only resigning; he was going as far away

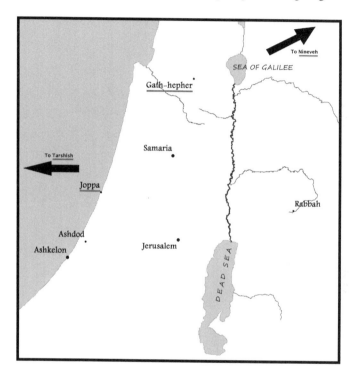

from the service of God as he possibly could!

One author put this into geographical perspective, stating that this would be like the word of the Lord coming to a Jewish man living in New York during World War II, commanding him to go to Berlin and deliver a warning of judgment from God to Nazi Germany. Instead of obeying, however, he drives from New York to San Francisco and then boards a ship bound for Hong Kong.[9]

Evidently Jonah cashed in his prophet's pension and came up with enough money to buy a one-way ticket. His mind was made up. He would sail to a faraway place where he would quietly live out the rest of his days.

Just look at Jonah run!

LESSONS FROM A PRODIGAL PROPHET

Three lessons strike me as I observe the prophet running from this difficult assignment from God.

1. Whenever we run from God in disobedience, we're always heading in the wrong direction.

Imagine Jonah down at the docks looking for a ship headed anywhere west. Gasping for breath, he runs down a boardwalk, asking captains and crewmembers alike, "Where are you heading? Egypt—no, that's too close to home. Antioch—no, no. Carthage—not there either."

Finally, he finds a captain and asks, "Sir, to where are you sailing? Tarshish? Tarshish—that's as far west as you can safely sail. That's perfect! How much?"

Can you imagine Jonah making his way to the shipping office to book passage and then paying the fare with coins stamped with the image of King Jeroboam II? Was Jonah smitten with guilt—even momentarily as those coins left his hand?

Had Jonah even told King Jeroboam he was leaving—and why? And what about Jonah's friends and family, people who counted on him, the young prophets who looked up to him, and a nation who heard God speak through him? Did he even leave a note?

There is so much wrong in not doing right. There are so many people affected by one person's sin; so much is lost.

2. Whenever we run from God in disobedience, we pay a higher price than we planned.

When we run from God, we can never find a place we can enjoy.

"Okay, I'm here . . . but why don't I feel better?"

The disobedient Christian is the most miserable person on the planet.

A generation ago Alexander Whyte noted in his commentary, "No booking clerk [in Joppa] could have told Jonah what it was actually going to cost him to get on board that ship. Running from God is always a costly affair."[10]

The old saying is still true:

- Sin will take you farther than you ever want to go.
- Sin will keep you longer than you ever want to stay.
- Sin will cost you more than you ever want to pay.

3. Whenever we run from God in disobedience, Satan will be happy to arrange the transportation.

Jonah was probably thinking how well everything was working out: "There just happens to be a ship that just happens to be about to weigh anchor, and it just so happens to be going far away from Nineveh. This is working out much easier than I imagined!"

What he never considered was the Enemy's delight in his disobedience. Nothing could have thrilled Satan more than to see Jonah safely tucked away in Tarshish, resigned in his disobedience to the will of God.

Anytime you want to run from God, expect transportation to be readily available.

For now, Jonah's lungs were filling with fresh air and sea breezes. But he had disobeyed some imperatives from God: "Arise . . . go . . . speak."

Have you ever thought about the fact that the Christian life is filled with imperatives—commands from God—that are clear, challenging, unmistakable, and unavoidable?

Consider these imperatives that are nonnegotiable commands:

- Follow Christ – John 12:26
- Speak the truth – Ephesians 4:25
- Put on the new self – Ephesians 4:24
- Be alert – Ephesians 6:18
- Flee immorality – 1 Corinthians 6:18
- Pray with thanksgiving – Philippians 4:6
- Sing with gratitude to God – Colossians 3:16
- Study the Word – 2 Timothy 2:15

And that's just the beginning. Jonah disobeyed three imperatives and ran the other way. What are we doing with *dozens* of imperatives? Have we set our sights on some distant Tarshish where we hope to avoid the hard commands and the difficult demands from the Lord? Are we running in the opposite direction?

At this moment Jonah thought *he* was in control. He had made it on board—disobedient, yes, but free from that last, awful assignment. God would just have to choose another prophet.

Exhausted from the hurried packing, the frenzied decisions, and a frantic race to the coast, he boarded a ship and soon fell fast asleep below deck. He falsely believed his disobedience would not matter to God all that much and that he had successfully retired from his prophetic role.

The words of one author summarize the issue and how Jonah should have responded to God's unusually difficult command. "I am not the master of my destiny—not even my daily life; God is. To obey means to yield my will for His will; my desire for His desire; to engage in activity that is different, or unpleasant, or strange, or dangerous, or difficult, or simply a drudge. I relinquish control . . . Another calls the shots . . . I am no longer my own master."[11]

Jonah might not have slept so soundly had he been able to see through the flooring of his cabin down into the deep waters of the Mediterranean Sea. Far below the ship a creature was swimming quietly, keeping pace, under orders to just tag along.[12]

Unlike Jonah, this creature will obey *every* command from its Creator God.

4The Lord hurled a great wind on the sea and there was a great storm on the sea so that the ship was about to break up. 5Then the sailors became afraid and every man cried to his god, and they threw the cargo which was in the ship into the sea to lighten it for them. But Jonah had gone below into the hold of the ship, lain down and fallen sound asleep. 6So the captain approached him and said, "How is it that you are sleeping? Get up, call on your god. Perhaps your god will be concerned about us so that we will not perish." 7Each man said to his mate, "Come, let us cast lots so we may learn on whose account this calamity has struck us." So they cast lots and the lot fell on Jonah. 8Then they said to him, "Tell us, now! On whose account has this calamity struck us? What is your occupation? And where do you come from? What is your country? From what people are you?" 9He said to them, "I am a Hebrew, and I fear the Lord God of heaven who made the sea and the dry land." 10Then the men became extremely frightened and they said to him, "How could you do this?" For the men knew that he was fleeing from the presence of the Lord, because he had told them. 11So they said to him, "What should we do to you that the sea may become calm for us?"—for the sea was becoming increasingly stormy. 12He said to them, "Pick me up and throw me into the sea. Then the sea will become calm for you, for I know that on account of me this great storm has come upon you." 13However, the men rowed desperately to return to land but they could not, for the sea was becoming even stormier against them. 14Then they called on the Lord and said, "We earnestly pray, O Lord, do not let us perish on account of this man's life and do not put innocent blood on us; for You, O Lord, have done as You have pleased." 15So they picked up Jonah, threw him into the sea, and the sea stopped its raging. 16Then the men feared the Lord greatly, and they offered a sacrifice to the Lord and made vows.

—Jonah 1:4–16

CHAPTER THREE

SEE JONAH SLEEP

Jonah 1:4–16

W hen a man decided to go to a Cincinnati Reds baseball game with his girlfriend, he knew he was running from the law. He had already broken parole—no one knew where he was. To further compound the problem, he had recently failed to appear in court to face drug charges.

During the game, the "Kiss Cam" went to work, spotting David and his girlfriend as they kissed, and their picture went up on the big screen for 30,000 people to see—including his parole officer who happened to be in the crowd! Before the game ended, the man was in handcuffs.[1]

As he ran in the opposite direction, the prophet of God evidently was under the impression he could hide from the surveillance lens of an omnipresent God. We can summarize what has happened thus far in one simple sentence: God said, "Go," and Jonah said, "No."

God effectively said, "I want you to go to Nineveh and deliver a message of mercy." And Jonah responded, "I'd rather resign than see the Ninevites repent."

With that, Jonah turned in his prophet's badge and hospital pass card, took the fish sticker off his carriage bumper, gave all his manuscripts to some younger prophet who might preach them, and headed for the coast of Spain—the exact opposite direction from Nineveh. Jonah would soon discover that God had not accepted his resignation.

What happens next in chapter 1 can be divided into three dramatic scenes:

- Scene One: Don't Disturb!
- Scene Two: Don't Ask!
- Scene Three: Don't Turn Around

SCENE ONE: DON'T DISTURB

Scene one opens in Jonah 1:4.

> **The Lord hurled a great wind on the sea and there was a great storm on the sea so that the ship was about to break up.**

With vivid horror, the text could be translated, "The Lord picked up a great wind and hurled it to the sea."[2]

> **Then the sailors became afraid and every man cried to his god.** (Jonah 1:5)

The Hebrew text for this verse could be translated, "Then each of the sailors shouted to his own god in prayer."[3] A spontaneous prayer meeting of extremely terrified sailors broke out on deck.

The word translated **sailors** comes from the Hebrew noun for *salt*. To this day, an old fisherman or sailor is called an "old salt."[4] These men were veteran sailors; they had ridden the high seas, and they knew storms. But *this* storm was so sudden and severe they assumed it would take a god to get them out of it alive. They were right.

Verse 5 also tells us:

> **Jonah had gone below into the hold of the ship, lain down and fallen sound asleep.**

Pagans were praying, and the prophet was sleeping. The prayers on deck were punctuated by the sound of cargo being heaved overboard to lighten the vessel.

Jonah heard none of it, for he was **sound asleep.** The Septuagint—the Greek translation of the Old Testament—translates the verb here as *snoring*. Jonah was literally snoring away, and that is probably how the captain located him.[5]

Several years ago a major hurricane swept through our area. The next morning my wife informed me that I had slept soundly through the entire ordeal—high winds, pelting rain, and falling trees. I slept through it all . . . that has to be a spiritual gift. And what a great way to ride out a storm!

Jonah had a "Do Not Disturb" sign hanging on his doorknob for the sailors to see. Worse yet, he had a "Do Not Disturb" sign hanging on his heart for God to see. In the meantime, he was snoring through the storm of the century.

> **So the captain approached him and said, "How is it that you are sleeping? Get up, call on your god."** (Jonah 1:6)

Literally, the captain was asking, "How is it that you can sleep through this storm?" He then ordered Jonah to **get up** and pray to his **god**.

When faced with natural disasters, it's amazing how quickly pagans can become prayer warriors. Suddenly these old salts were offering up supplications, convinced some deity was behind the storm.

Wanting to make sure he had every god covered, the captain pulled Jonah off his bunk and barked, "Wake up, man! Start praying to whatever god you believe in."

Then, for the first time, Jonah felt the reeling and rocking of the boat; he heard the wind howling and felt the shuddering of the timber under his feet and immediately sensed their mortal danger. More than that, he immediately knew which god was behind the storm—*his* God. He had run from God, and God had been waiting on the high seas for him to arrive.

God is always ahead of us, behind us, above us, beside us, and beneath us. Wherever we run, He's already there.

Jonah was the only man on board who knew the true and living God, but at the moment, he wasn't exactly on speaking terms with Him. Still, Jonah could hear the voice of God in the howling wind.[6]

Let's make one more observation from Scene One. The captain says at the end of verse 6:

> **"Perhaps your god will be concerned about us so that we will not perish."**

It's interesting that pagans will often hold the believer to a higher standard than the believer will hold himself.

This captain effectively was urging Jonah, "Maybe your god will feel sorry for us . . . pray that he will spare us in mercy."

Don't miss the irony here. This old salt delivered words that were like salt to Jonah's prodigal heart. The very thing Jonah did not want God to do for the pagan Ninevites was the very thing he was being asked to pray for on behalf of these pagan sailors.

Jonah had resigned from the service of God because he did not want God to show mercy to the Ninevites. Now he was in the middle of a storm that threatened to sink the ship, and he was being asked to pray that God would show mercy to all those on board.

Still, Jonah would *not* pray. There's no reference to any petition offered on behalf of the crew or the ship. The prodigal prophet was evidently sticking with his "Do Not Disturb" sign. His unspoken answer was, "Don't bother me. Leave me alone. Ask somebody else for help."

The second scene now opens, and the camera shifts our focus from below deck to above deck.

SCENE 2: DON'T ASK!

The prayer meeting wasn't working, so the sailors moved to something they were more familiar with—throwing dice.

> **Each man said to his mate, "Come, let us cast lots so we may learn on whose account this calamity has struck us." So they cast lots and the lot fell on Jonah.** (Jonah 1:7)

These dice, or **lots**, were often small stones. The corresponding Arabic word means *pebbles*. History records that colored balls or pieces of wood of varying lengths were used for casting lots.[7] The person with the longest piece of wood or the colored stone was the winner. Whatever form these lots took didn't matter—Jonah won.

As soon as the lot identified Jonah as the cause of the storm, he was besieged with a flurry of questions.

> **Then they said to him, "Tell us, now! On whose account has this calamity struck us? What is your occupation? And where do you come from? What is your country? From what people are you?"** (Jonah 1:8)

Imagine this scene. The wind is whipping across the deck, and the ship is rolling up and down on huge waves. The rain-drenched sailors, hardly able to stand, throw pebbles, and the stranger who kept to himself and strangely slept through the storm wins the draw.

The sailors' first question could be rendered, "What have you done?" This was followed by a second question: **"What is your occupation?"** That question was one Jonah didn't want to answer because he was actually running from his occupation!

Jonah probably couldn't believe what was happening. God simply would not leave him alone—the prophet had been pinned down in the middle of the sea.

The implications of the sailors' questions were clear. We can imagine them saying, "Jonah, it's obviously your god who is upset. What did you do to bring this on? What do you do for a living?"

Jonah could no longer say with authority and conviction, "I am a prophet of God." In fact, he had no word from God to offer.

It's a wonderful thing when you are doing something right and somebody asks, "Hey, are you by any chance a Christian?"

But have you ever done something wrong and somebody said to you, "Hey, I thought you were a Christian."

It is tragic when a believer's sin is exposed to the watching world.

Jonah finally answered:

> **"I am a Hebrew, and I fear the Lord God of heaven who made the sea and the dry land."** (Jonah 1:9)

Jonah remained composed, as if he were on the good side of God. But don't miss this: Jonah's answer is perfect theology but utter hypocrisy. **"I am a Hebrew,"** he said. That was true enough. He identified the Lord as the maker of **the sea and the dry land**. That is sound theology.

According to a *Chicago Sun-Times* article, Nita Friedman did not seem the type of person to be involved in a police pursuit, but she was. After Police Chief Mike Hutter attempted to pull her over for a traffic violation, she refused to stop. Even after the chief flipped on his lights and siren, instead of pulling over, this sixty-six-year-old woman pulled away. Police followed her through three counties, and the chase did not end until the state police put a spike strip in the road in front of Friedman's car. After driving over the strip and having three of her tires go flat, she tried to keep going. Escape became impossible, however, and she finally pulled over and stopped.

What astounded the police was that throughout the entire ordeal, Ms. Friedman never exceeded the speed limit. She observed all the traffic laws, even stopping at one point behind a vehicle that was making a left turn. What irony—while running from the law, this woman was determined not to break the law.[8]

Likewise, Jonah was trying *not* to discredit God, while at the same time disobeying God. He was careful to acknowledge that Yahweh is the God of the land and sea, while at the same time attempting to flee from Him by land and sea.

These sailors were able to pull more out of Jonah than this simple admission, however.

> **Then the men became extremely frightened and they said to him, "How could you do this?" For the men knew that he was fleeing from the presence of the Lord, because he had told them.** (Jonah 1:10)

When they learned he was fleeing from God, they erupted, shouting at him, **"How could you do this?"**

What a tragedy it is when pagans have more clarity than prophets and when the world exposes the sins Christians had hoped to hide.

SCENE THREE: DON'T TURN AROUND!

> **So they said to him, "What should we do to you that the sea may become calm for us?"—for the sea was becoming increasingly stormy.** (Jonah 1:11)

The storm was bad before; now it was growing worse. The sailors pleaded with Jonah to tell them what they should do.

What these pagans missed was Jonah's motive. They thought he was running away from God because of something he had *done*. They did not know he was running away from God because of something he would *not do*. They thought Jonah had done something *wrong*, when in reality he had refused to do something *right*.

Jonah stunned them by offering this solution:

"Pick me up and throw me into the sea. Then the sea will become calm for you, for I know that on account of me this great storm has come upon you." (Jonah 1:12)

Underlying his answer was Jonah's determination not to go back to Nineveh. The prophet would rather die in the sea than repent and go to the Assyrian city and represent a merciful God.

Frankly, we would expect these pagan sailors to immediately pick up Jonah and toss him into the waves. After all, they wanted to live to sail another day. Instead:

The men rowed desperately to return to land but they could not, for the sea was becoming even stormier against them. (Jonah 1:13)

The **men rowed desperately** in an attempt to reach land. The Hebrew phrase indicates that they literally dug in with all their might to save not only their lives, but also Jonah's life.

Again, do not miss the irony in this. Jonah would not lift a finger to save the lives of pagan Ninevites, but these idol-worshiping sailors put their lives on the line to save his. Can you imagine how convicted this prodigal prophet felt as these unbelievers risked their lives to save him, while his own refusal to help thousands had endangered these sailors as well as himself.

Their rowing was of no use, so the sailors in desperation prayed to Yahweh.

They called on the Lord and said, "We earnestly pray, O Lord, do not let us perish on account of this man's life and do not put innocent blood on us; for You, O Lord, have done as You have pleased." (Jonah 1:14)

This is an incredibly perceptive prayer from a group of pagan sailors. There was something happening in their lives, which we will come back to in a moment. In the meantime, we read:

They picked up Jonah, threw him into the sea, and the sea stopped its raging. (Jonah 1:15)

Notice that Jonah did not repent. There was no quick prayer of confession. There was no request that the ship be turned around and he be allowed to follow God in obedience. He was resigned to die in his stubborn, defiant state.

What an incredible downward spiral in Jonah's life. He had once thought the Ninevites should not be allowed to live; now he was willing to end his life. Rather than surrender to God, he would forfeit his own life.

The average Christian might not face such a dramatic decision. But when we walk away from obedience to God, we cease living the kind of life that is worth living. We forfeit a full reward (2 John 8).

Prodigals waste their potential. As far as the prodigal prophet was concerned, he would rather die than see the Ninevites repent and find true life.

As soon as Jonah's body hit the water, the sea became calm.

Then the men feared the Lord greatly. (Jonah 1:16)

Jonah said earlier that he **feared the Lord**, but he really did not. Now these sailors were confessing that they **feared the Lord greatly,** and look at what it led them to do. The rest of verse 16 records:

They offered a sacrifice to the Lord and made vows.

This phrase can be understood to mean they *promised to serve Him* or *they vowed to serve Him*, indicating genuine conversion to the God of Israel.[9] Thus this scene closes with even greater irony. Jonah refused to keep his prophetic vows to worship and serve God, but these converted pagans are making vows to worship and serve God.

This was no foxhole conversion. Mark the fact that these vows were made, not during the storm as a promise that they would convert *if* the storm ended, but *after* the storm was over.[10] After the sailors had been delivered, they promised to serve God and God alone.

Imagine this revival—and Jonah missed it. Prodigals miss the blessings of God's Spirit because they are focused on having their own way. There are *two* revivals in this book, and Jonah misses them both.

From all appearances, Jonah has been discarded—dumped overboard like cheap cargo. Truly, when we choose to defy God, our lives are ultimately cheapened.

THE GRACE OF GOD

Not quite as noticeable, the grace of God was still at work in Jonah's life in at least two ways.

- **First, even when Jonah was disobedient, God used his words to reveal His glory.**

Who would have ever thought the conversion of these pagan sailors was even possible? This is the revival most often overlooked in this little book. Hardened sailors became dedicated servants of God.

In spite of himself, Jonah was actually used by God as a messenger of the glory and grace of God.

- **Second, even when Jonah was discarded by these sailors, he was not discarded by God.**

God had a special fish ready and waiting for His prodigal prophet. Had I been God, I would have sent a shark—a big one. I might have allowed Jonah to live, but I would have made sure he had teeth marks so he'd never forget. And I would've gone looking for another prophet.

The good news is that while Jonah wanted to forget about God, God had not forgotten about Jonah. Jonah had given up. God had not.

I imagine as Jonah hit that cold water of the Mediterranean Sea, he more than likely thought, "What a way to go . . . I've blown it. . . . there's no hope for me now. . . . I'll never see the light of day again."

Jonah was about to be surprised by a gracious God who faithfully loves even prodigal sons.

Suddenly, the lights were turned out as Jonah felt himself being swept downward in a strange current. Just as quickly, the water dissipated as his feet touched strange, slippery ground. He knew he was alive because he could hear his heart beating . . . he was still breathing. Where in the world was he?

What Jonah assumed would be the end of his life was only the end of an unfortunate chapter. This was actually the *beginning* of a new chapter, and it would be written in a most unusual place.

1:17 And the Lord appointed a great fish to swallow Jonah, and Jonah was in the stomach of the fish three days and three nights. 2:1 Then Jonah prayed to the Lord his God from the stomach of the fish, 2and he said, "I called out of my distress to the Lord, and He answered me. I cried for help from the depth of Sheol; You heard my voice. 3For You had cast me into the deep, into the heart of the seas, and the current engulfed me. All Your breakers and billows passed over me. 4So I said, 'I have been expelled from Your sight. Nevertheless I will look again toward Your holy temple.' 5Water encompassed me to the point of death. The great deep engulfed me, weeds were wrapped around my head. 6I descended to the roots of the mountains. The earth with its bars was around me forever, but You have brought up my life from the pit, O Lord my God. 7While I was fainting away, I remembered the Lord, and my prayer came to You, into Your holy temple. 8Those who regard vain idols forsake their faithfulness, 9but I will sacrifice to You with the voice of thanksgiving. That which I have vowed I will pay. Salvation is from the Lord." 10Then the Lord commanded the fish, and it vomited Jonah up onto the dry land.

Jonah 1:17–2:10

CHAPTER FOUR

SEE JONAH SWIM

Jonah 1:17–2:10

O f all the passages in the Bible that have raised questions about the truthfulness of Scripture, Jonah and the great fish would have to rank high on the list. A woman who joined our fellowship wrote in her testimony of faith how her struggle with the truth actually converged at the book of Jonah. She wrote:

> Twenty years ago, as an unsaved Catholic, I was preparing to teach my Sunday school class what the church calls, "The Children's Liturgy of the Word." The lesson for that Sunday was about Jonah and the whale. The church curriculum explained that the Catholic Church believed it was *not* a true story. "The Children's Liturgy of the Word" simply told it as a story used by God to teach a lesson on obedience.

When I read this, I couldn't help but wonder, just what would that lesson be? If you disobey God, don't go near the water? If you've sinned against God, you'd better not go fishing?

She continued:

> As I taught this lesson to my own children on Saturday night (for practice), my unsaved Presbyterian husband walked past and overheard me and said, "Of course that story is true!" He believed it! With that brief comment, God initiated in me a desire to know what was true.

I prayed and asked the Lord to show me the truth, and several months later while in my car, I heard a creation scientist explaining how the geology of the earth defended the great flood of Noah—something else my church had told me was "just another story." My spirit was suddenly overwhelmed with an inner confirmation that the Word of God—all of it—is true.

This woman went on to write how a few months later, again through Christian radio, she heard a clear gospel message and accepted Christ alone as her Savior. "Jonah and the Whale" became the point of crisis that eventually led her to repentance.

We are about to see that same whale bringing someone else to a point of crisis that also led to repentance.

THE TRUTH OF JONAH AND THE WHALE

We last saw Jonah sinking into the Mediterranean Sea and then disappearing in one gulp as the lights went out around him.

And the Lord appointed a great fish to swallow Jonah, and Jonah was in the stomach of the fish three days and three nights. (Jonah 1:17)

Without a doubt, this is one of the most maligned verses in the Bible; this fish has been examined by more theologians than any other fish to swim the seven seas, and the imagination so many of them have exercised to keep Jonah out of the literal belly of a literal fish is literally amazing.

One author suggested that what actually happened was another ship, named *The Fish,* happened to come by and rescue Jonah before he drowned.[1] Another suggested that Jonah swam to dry ground and then stayed at an inn named, "The Fish," where he recuperated for three days and three nights.[2]

A generation ago skeptics were arguing that the throat of a whale was too small to even swallow an orange without difficulty. For some whales this is true. However, the examination and observations of the *average* sperm whale known to swim in the Mediterranean reveal that it has a throat twenty feet long, fifteen feet high, and nine feet wide.[3] That's large enough to swallow a mobile home!

Marine biologists also have determined that such a large fish would have enough air inside its stomach for someone to breathe, though the temperature would be a hot and humid 104 degrees Fahrenheit.

I came across some research provided by the *Princeton Theological Review* in a 1927 issue, which reported on a case that occurred in 1891. The whaling ship *Star of the East* was hunting in the vicinity of the Falkland Islands, when the fishermen spotted a large sperm whale. Two smaller boats were sent after it. One was able to harpoon the whale, but those in the second boat capsized in the process, and one man drowned. A second sailor, James Bartley, disappeared and could not be found. In time the whale was killed and drawn to the side of the ship, where it was secured and divided. The following day the stomach was separated from the carcass and hoisted on deck; when it was opened, the missing sailor was found inside; unconscious, bleached white, and still alive. He was revived and after some time resumed his duties on board the vessel.[4]

Frankly, we don't need a story from the *Princeton Theological Review* to help us believe Jonah was swallowed by the great fish and survived. All we need is the record of Scripture, which without apology—and, interestingly, without detailed explanation—simply states, **the Lord appointed a great fish to swallow Jonah.**

God had prepared a fish for the job. The question is not, "Is there a fish big enough to swallow Jonah alive?" The question is, "Is there a God big enough to create and command a whale?" If God is for real, the fish part is easy.

Don't miss the descriptive phrase, **the Lord appointed.** This word can also be translated, *prepared, assigned,* or *commanded.*

This was the first biblical reference to a fish being given an assignment from God. But it would not be the last time. The Lord commanded a fish to hold a shekel in its mouth—a coin about the size of a nickel. Then the Lord commanded that fish to take Peter's bait when Peter put his hook into the water. The Lord had told Peter that the first fish he caught would have the money in its mouth needed to pay their taxes (Matthew 17:27).

Now, that's my kind of fishing!

The Lord also commanded ravens to carry bread to Elijah as he hid by the brook Cherith (1 Kings 17:6).

Fish do not carry money around in their mouths, and birds do not bring bread to strangers—unless they have been *appointed by God.*

Throughout the book of Jonah, we see God giving assignments to various things He created. This same Hebrew verb—translated **appointed**—appears five times.

- The first one is here, as the Lord *appointed* a fish to swallow and sustain Jonah (1:17).

- The second time is when this same fish is *commanded* to spit Jonah out (2:10).

- The third time is when God *appointed* a plant to grow up quickly (4:6).

- Then the Lord *appointed* a worm to destroy the plant (4:7).

- Finally, the Lord *appointed* a hot east wind to blow against Jonah (4:8).

The same Hebrew concept is communicated in all five occasions. All were assigned, or commanded, by their Creator, and they all obeyed. Without exception they fulfilled their assignment from God.

Would Jonah get the message?

Jonah 1:17 simply announces,

> **The Lord appointed a great fish to swallow Jonah, and Jonah was in the stomach of the fish three days and three nights.**

As Jonah dropped down into the belly of the great fish, felt the great heat, and breathed the putrid air, he realized where he was. At the same time, he was no doubt fully aware he had little hope and was beyond help. God was allowing Jonah to experience a taste of what the Ninevites would experience in judgment—hopelessness and helplessness.[5]

JONAH'S UNDERWATER PRAYER

Chapter 2 of Jonah opens with these words:

> **Then Jonah prayed to the Lord his God.**

I imagine he did!

We are not told exactly *when* Jonah prayed. Was it after he swirled into the fish's mouth, or was it when he slid down its gullet and landed in the dark cavern of its belly? We're not told.

Some scholars believe Jonah did not pray at first. In fact, some Hebrew scholars believe the text implies Jonah did not pray until the third day.

What we *do* know is that it is possible to become so fascinated with the fish that we overlook what happened in the heart of Jonah—a prodigal who *finally* prayed.

This is the only prayer in history ever recorded under water. We will discover in Jonah's prayer three critical ingredients of genuine repentance.

1. **Admission is the first ingredient of Jonah's prayer of repentance.**

   He said, "I called out of my distress to the Lord, and He answered me. I cried for help from the depth of Sheol [the grave]; You heard my voice. For You had cast me into the deep, into the heart of the seas, and the current engulfed me. All Your breakers and billows passed over me." (Jonah 2:2–3)

As Jonah called out to the Lord from the belly of the fish, he admitted that the distress he was experiencing was God's hand of discipline.

Hebrews 12:5–9 provides a New Testament counterpart to this kind of admission. According to this text, we can respond to God's discipline in one of four ways:

- We can despise God's discipline and fight it (v. 5*a*).
- We can be discouraged and faint because of it (v. 5*b*).
- We can resist and invite more of it (v. 9).
- Or we can submit and grow because of it (v. 7).[6]

At this point Jonah was no longer resisting the will of God or rejecting the word of God. In fact, he was about to reenlist in the work of God. The first step was admission of wrong and the right of God to discipline.

   "So I said, 'I have been expelled from Your sight.'" (Jonah 2:4*a*)

Up to this point, Jonah's focus had been in the opposite direction of God's authority. In fact, the word that best characterizes the life of Jonah up to this point is the word *down*.

- Jonah rose up to flee and went *down* to Joppa, the seaport
- Jonah paid the fare and went *down* into the ship.
- Then he was swallowed by the great fish, effectively going *down* into its belly.
- Now Jonah was going *down* into the deep abyss of the sea.

When you turn your back on God, the only direction you can go is down.[7]

2. The second ingredient of Jonah's prayer of repentance is restoration.

"'Nevertheless I will look again toward Your holy temple.'"
(Jonah 2:4*b*)

Once Jonah admitted his sin, he was on his way to restoration. He, in fact, turned his spiritual gaze toward the **temple** of God. This was a statement of recommitment for the Old Testament saint, taken from Solomon's prayer of dedication when the temple was completed. In that great prayer, Solomon had said,

> Whatever prayer or supplication is made by any man or by all Your people Israel, each knowing the affliction of his own heart, and spreading his hands toward this house; then hear in heaven Your dwelling place, and forgive and act and render to each according to all his ways, whose heart You know, for You alone know the hearts of all the sons of men. (1 Kings 8:38–39)

Jonah was literally clinging to this promise in repentance and faith. And God responded accordingly:

> **"Water encompassed me to the point of death. The great deep engulfed me, weeds were wrapped around my head. I descended to the roots of the mountains. The earth with its bars was around me forever."** (Jonah 2:5–6*a*)

In other words, there was no escape. Jonah believed he was going to die. Yet Jonah continued in faith:

> **"But You have brought up my life from the pit, O Lord my God."** (Jonah 2:6*b*)

Earlier, on deck, Jonah would not even pray. He was running from God and unwilling to speak for God. He would not even pray to God on behalf of the terrified sailors who were afraid of drowning. Now, however, he remembered the Lord: **"You have brought up my life from the pit, O Lord my God."** Jonah continued:

> **"While I was fainting away, I remembered the Lord, and my prayer came to You into Your holy temple."** (Jonah 2:7)

He was without hope—and then he **remembered the Lord**. Sinclair Ferguson writes, "Isn't it marvelous that God has mercy on Jonah *before* Jonah will preach that God will have mercy on Nineveh."[8]

It is no wonder, then, that there is a final aspect of repentance, in addition to admission and restoration.

3. **Appreciation is the third ingredient of Jonah's prayer of repentance.**

Listen to Jonah pray:

> **"Those who regard vain idols forsake their faithfulness. But I will sacrifice to You, with the voice of thanksgiving. That which I have vowed I will pay. Salvation is from the Lord."** (Jonah 2:8–9)

Keep in mind that Jonah had not been given a promise of deliverance from his watery grave. Jonah was not thankful because he was back on dry land; he was thankful that God had turned his heart from rebellion and caused him to call on the name of the Lord once again.[9] The last phrase in Jonah's prayer of repentance announced a breathtaking revelation, or reminder, to his heart and mind. **Salvation is from the Lord** was not so much a theological declaration as it was a personal confession of faith.

In expressing his appreciation to the true God, Jonah contrasted himself with those who followed **vain idols**. He promised to sacrifice to God and pay his vows. He used the same vocabulary the sailors had used earlier when they also repented and claimed the God of Israel as their personal God. There on that sea-washed deck, they indeed sacrificed animals and vowed to serve God.

But how could Jonah offer a **sacrifice**? He could not sacrifice an animal—he had been swallowed by one! It seems he had gone too far. What vow could he possibly offer to God?

Jonah could offer to God the same thing you and I can offer Him.

In David's great hymn of repentance, he wrote,

> The sacrifices of God are a broken spirit; a broken and a contrite heart, O God, You will not despise. (Psalm 51:17)

No matter how far you have run from God and no matter where you are right now, the Enemy will say to you, "You've gone too far. Why would God want you back? You have nothing now to offer Him."

This is a lie. You can offer to God the sacrifices He loves most—the sacrifices of a broken spirit and a contrite heart.

As Jonah offered up to God the sacrifices of a repentant heart and a humbled spirit, God responded by sending upon the great fish the biggest case of indigestion any creature has ever experienced. Suddenly, that great fish simply couldn't keep Jonah down.

Then the Lord commanded the fish, and it vomited Jonah up onto the dry land. (Jonah 2:10)

The fish could not digest the prophet and at God's command, he spit him up onto dry land.

That must have gathered a crowd.

The prodigal prophet had returned, by whale express, home again and back to the service of his Lord God.

CONCLUSION

Lois Krueger tells a story about her son Carl when he was four and a half years old. Lois and her husband had been having one of those hectic weeks and their son just seemed to be getting into more and more trouble—getting in the way and causing problems. He was sent to the corner for time-out, and while in his confinement he suddenly piped up and said, "I'm gonna run away from home."

Lois stopped and remembered that moment from her own childhood when she felt the same way—always in trouble and in the way; never in the right; even a bit unloved.

She went over to her son and responded with unique wisdom, saying, "Okay, you can run away from home."

"I can?" he said.

"Yes," she responded, "you can. Come on, let's pack."

She pulled out his suitcase and then hers as well and began to pick out her clothes. He said, "Mama, what are you doing?"

She said, "Well, I'm going to need my coat and my pajamas and my shoes." She packed her things and placed the suitcase by the front door with his and said, "Okay, are you sure you want to run away from home?"

He said, "I am, but where are you going?"

She said, "Well, if you're going to run away from home, then Mama's going with you because I would never want you to be alone."[10]

How wise of this mother.

How infinitely wise and gracious is our heavenly Father. His prophet Jonah ran away; but when he was ready to call out to the Lord, he discovered that God had never left him alone.

Even in Jonah's darkest moments of despair—when the lights were extinguished and the prison bars of the deep abyss were telling him, "There's no way out of this; there's no way back; you're alone, and you're finished"— God was present. And even in the darkness of the fish, Jonah experienced communion with the God he had offended and the Lord he had spurned. Even in that abyss, the goodness of God led him to repentance.

Jonah was revived, restored, and reenlisted in God's service.

No matter how long we stay silent, God will hear us whenever we're ready to talk. And we discover in those moments of reviving grace that when we ran away in sinful rebellion, the Lord came along with us.

The most amazing miracle in Jonah 2 is not the preservation of Jonah inside a fish but the restoration inside Jonah's heart.

There deep down in the Mediterranean Sea . . . down in the belly of a whale, the prodigal prophet actually came *home*.

[1]Now the word of the Lord came to Jonah the second time, saying, [2]"Arise, go to Nineveh the great city and proclaim to it the proclamation which I am going to tell you." [3]So Jonah arose and went to Nineveh according to the word of the Lord. Now Nineveh was an exceedingly great city, a three days' walk. [4]Then Jonah began to go through the city one day's walk; and he cried out and said, "Yet forty days and Nineveh will be overthrown."

–Jonah 3:1–4

CHAPTER FIVE

SEE JONAH PREACH

Jonah 3:1–4

Every year my hometown region hosts the North Carolina State Fair. I usually attend for one reason, and that reason can be stated in two words: *deep fried.*

After I eat an oversized corn on the cob to get my vegetables out of the way, I go to my favorite vendor and stand in line for an hour. But it's worth it for the deep-fried Snickers candy bar. A stick is poked through the Snickers—sort of like a corndog. It is dipped into what looks like pancake batter and then transferred over to a vat of oil, where it is deep-fried. After a few seconds it comes out fluffy and crispy. The well-trained "chef" then rolls it in powdered sugar and hands it to me as I stand there drooling. I can almost hear my left aorta slamming shut.

A few years ago I tried the deep-fried Twinkie, but it was really too sweet. I have my standards!

It's hard to believe we are selling stuff like this—and eating it—at the same time our culture is becoming more and more aware of fat grams and bad cholesterol. In fact, restaurants are being held liable now for cooking with trans fat.

Trans fat is created by pumping hydrogen into oil at high temperatures. It creates not only an inexpensive fat product for cooking but also prolongs shelf life in products. It also creates—so they advertise—"food that is flavorful and crisp." No doubt that is why we want to eat it.

Some states are now banning restaurants from using it. One can only wonder how long it will take before this conspiracy reaches the North

Carolina State Fair. Any year may be my last opportunity to enjoy a crisp, flavorful deep-fried Snickers.

If junk food like that was sold only at the State Fair, we would all be better off. In fact, I'm glad I don't have the option of eating that stuff but once a year.

The trouble, however, is that "junk food" is not just a physical temptation—it's also a spiritual problem.

Walter Kaiser pointed out the anemic state of affairs in the American church today, and he placed the responsibility squarely on the shoulders of pastors and teachers who are preaching and teaching everything but the Word of God. He writes:

> It is no secret that Christ's church is not at all in good health. . . . She has been languishing because she has been fed, as the current line has it, "junk food"; all kinds of artificial preservatives and all sorts of unnatural substitutes have been served up to her. As a result, theological and Biblical malnutrition has afflicted the very generation that has taken such giant steps to make sure its physical health is never damaged by using foods or products that are . . . harmful to their physical bodies. Simultaneously a spiritual famine resulting from the absence of any genuine publication of the Word of God (Amos 8:11) continues to run wild.[1]

Unfortunately, the average church is serving up deep-fried sermons, Sunday school lessons, and Bible study materials. There is little spiritual nutrition. It is artificially sweet and without textual substance or theological fiber. There is no meat in sight. Creative topics and superficial sermon series, skipping here and there for quick answers and clever fixes, have left the church in poor spiritual health.

The solution is not a ban on unhealthy things. The solution is a change of diet; it is a return to teaching, not just the Word of God in general, but also *every* word of God.

While pastors, Sunday school teachers, and Bible study leaders will be tempted to simply teach on the latest interest about life in general, they must resist that temptation for the sake of the church's health. It bears repeating that the average ministry is expounding on life and illustrating with Scripture, but we must return to expounding *Scripture* and illustrating with life.

By the time most Christians reach Jonah chapter 3, they are under the impression that all the action is over. They might have some faint awareness that Nineveh repented and Jonah was not too happy about it, but once they get past the great fish throwing Jonah up onto dry land, that about wraps up the series for them and it's time to move on to another Bible story.

Actually, Jonah 3 holds the key to a spiritual awakening—a return to spiritual health and vitality that begins in the pulpit and spreads throughout the church. We are in desperate need today for preachers and teachers to follow the example of Jonah—and for people to respond like the Ninevites.

JONAH'S FIRST CHANCE

You will remember that the Lord had told Jonah to go to Nineveh, but instead, he went down to Joppa on the coast of the Mediterranean and booked passage on a ship heading for Tarshish, which was on the coast of Spain. Tarshish was in the opposite direction, as far from Nineveh as Jonah could travel.

Why did Jonah do this? One reason is that he was a patriotic Jew. He had come to believe, as most of his countrymen had, that God exclusively belonged to *them*—that salvation belonged to the Jewish people.

Only when he was inside the fish did Jonah rediscover that **salvation is from the Lord** (Jonah 2:9). Salvation is His to give to whomever He desires to give it.

Furthermore Jonah was bitterly resentful, if not afraid, of the infamous cruelty of the Assyrians toward their captives. I was recently at the British Museum in London and saw firsthand the clay designs that once plastered the king's palace walls in Nineveh, featuring the drawings of prisoners being tortured and of piles of skulls stacked by castle walls.

Jonah did not want God to show mercy to this unmerciful people. He did not want them to receive anything from God but punishment and death, as he admitted later (Jonah 4:2). So he ran.

Following Jonah's rebellion, if I were God, I would have started looking for another prophet.

JONAH'S SECOND CHANCE

The opening line of chapter 3 is freighted with surprising grace.

Now the word of the Lord came to Jonah the second time.
(Jonah 3:1)

Pause for a moment and let the words sink in: **the second time.** What grace and forgiveness are bound up in those three wonderful words.

We would not reenlist someone like Jonah. We would go back to the drawing board. We would begin reviewing resumes. We would start over—with someone else. Peter had his chance in the courtyard. John Mark had his shot on the mission field with Paul. Thomas missed his chance by skipping out on the upper room. But they all were given second chances!

James Montgomery Boice wrote in his commentary on Jonah:

> If we were to say, "Go home now, Jonah. I'm glad you repent-
> ed of your disobedience, but you are no longer useful to me,"
> we would be just and reasonable in doing so. . . . Does God
> stoop to use those who have rejected His calling, turned a deaf
> ear to His word, and pursued a course of determined disobe-
> dience? Yes, He is like that. Yes, He does use such messengers.
> If He did not, none of us could serve Him.[2]

This is not defending disobedience. This is defending the grace of God—not just in Jonah's life but in your life and mine as well. He is the God of second chances and beyond.

Honest reflection compels the believer to speak of Him as the God of the 999th chance; how many times have we been forgiven and had yet another opportunity given to us to do something for Christ?[3]

Imagine the thrill of Jonah the prophet as he heard the word of the Lord coming to him again, **the second time.**

George Morrison, the well-known Scottish pastor and writer from several generations ago, once wrote, "The victorious Christian life is really nothing more than a series of new beginnings."[4]

JONAH'S SACRED CHARGE

"Arise, go to Nineveh the great city and proclaim to it the proclamation which I am going to tell you." (Jonah 3:2)

This is the same commission Jonah received in chapter 1. However, in that first commission God had rehearsed for Jonah the wickedness of the Ninevites. In this *second* commission, that part is omitted, and Jonah is simply challenged with the sacred task of proclaiming God's message.

This charge was nothing less than to preach God's word. It's the same charge given by Paul to Timothy and every pastor since: "Preach the word" (2 Timothy 4:2).

There will always be the pull to preach something else—something more appealing, something more titillating, something more positive or promising. Nonetheless, the reformation of souls and the awakening of hearts come by means of the power of the gospel (Romans 1:16), which comes through "the word of God [which] is living and active and sharper than any two-edged sword" (Hebrews 4:12).

There is something else in this recommission that can be understood as a subtle warning to Jonah. Jonah had just survived three days in the belly of a great fish; he had just traveled from the depths of the Mediterranean Sea to the place where the fish spit him out onto dry land.

Think about his sensational testimony! No one could top this one. His story would draw thousands of people! Imagine the crowds that would gather to hear:

- "My Miracle Ride in the Belly of a Fish"
- "How I Survived Three Days Underwater"
- "Life Inside a Whale and Why I'll Never Eat Fish Again"

Jonah's story would be a best seller in no time at all. He had experienced what no one else had and lived to tell about it.

But there is none of this in God's charge. God wasn't interested in Jonah telling his testimony of an underwater adventure. He simply tells Jonah to go to Nineveh and proclaim His message, as if to imply: "Don't tell your fish story, Jonah; don't dramatize your call back into ministry; don't sensationalize your experience; don't focus attention on yourself; just go to that great metropolis and deliver My word to them."

Four times in the book of Jonah Nineveh is referred to as a **great city** (1:2; 3:2; 3:3; 4:11).

- It was great in history, having been founded by Nimrod, the great-grandson of Noah (Genesis 10:8–11).

- It was great in size. The circumference of the city and its suburbs was about sixty miles, and it had a population of perhaps 600,000. One interior wall of the city had a circumference of eight miles and boasted 1500 towers.

- It was great in sin, being idolatrous, immoral, and brutal.[5]

Jonah would have entered Nineveh through a massive gate with towers stretching into the sky. Assyrian soldiers would have been looking down at this foreigner who dared to enter.

Jonah was likely given a personal audience with the king himself, who, the text implies, repented upon hearing the message. If so, Jonah would have seen the palace as it looked when it was excavated centuries later—brilliantly colored with battle scenes.

For years, skeptics argued that the Bible spoke of a great city called Nineveh when there was no extrabiblical evidence the city had even existed. Then in the mid-1800s, an archeologist named Austin Layard discovered the hill under which the buried ruins of Nineveh lay. The dry conditions had remarkably preserved this ancient city.

We now know Jonah would have entered the palace and stood near two huge oxen with wings and the faces of bearded men. These figures were placed in palaces and at the entrances of temples to supposedly protect the people from evil spirits. A pair of these winged gods were excavated by Layard and now stand in the British Museum. These stone statues, perfectly preserved over the course of three thousand years, may have been the same statues Jonah saw with his own eyes.

Winged bulls at the British Museum

These winged bulls with human heads and faces supposedly served the king of Nineveh as guardians to protect him from spiritual danger. I can imagine Jonah taking the opportunity to point at these massive idols and announce, "O King, these guardians will not protect you from the judgment of my true and living God. You have forty days until He judges you, your city, and your people."

Did the king listen? Frankly, I believe the king was already *prepared* to listen. In fact, Jonah might have been given nothing less than a royal reception. The text even seems to imply that Jonah was given assistance in order to travel from place to place, covering all the key places in the city in a very short period of time.

There is no reason to doubt that the story of Jonah riding in the belly of a great fish and being delivered to dry ground had already reached the ears of the king. And such a story would have had great impact in Nineveh. One of the chief gods of the Ninevites just happened to be the fish-god named Dagon (*dag* was the word for fish). The Ninevites worshiped Dagon in the belief that he ruled the Mediterranean Sea. This god was portrayed as a man from the waist up and a fish from the waist down. Carvings and paintings of Dagon have been discovered by archeologists in and around the city of Nineveh.

The fish-god Dagon

Add to this the fact that a Phoenician inscription from two hundred years after Jonah lived informs us that one of the chief cities of Dagon was Joppa, the very city from which Jonah departed on the ship and more than likely the very place he was returned to by the great fish.

Put all the pieces together, and it is little wonder why the Ninevites were prepared to listen. God used Jonah's disobedience and intentionally chose this unique form of transportation back to Joppa with the Ninevites' superstition and idolatry in mind. The Ninevites were prepared to listen to a prophet who rode inside a great fish that was under the command of Jonah's God—a God who was evidently more powerful than their great fish-god.

The stage was uniquely set for the greatest national conversion in the history of the planet.

> **Then Jonah began to go through the city one day's walk; and he cried out and said, "Yet forty days and Nineveh will be overthrown."** (Jonah 3:4)

The word **overthrow** means *to turn upside down*. The tense of the verb indicates thoroughness, emphasizing that this would be a *complete* destruction, or overturning, of the city's foundations, walls, and gates.

From a human perspective, Jonah's evangelistic enterprise appears ridiculous. How could one man, claiming to be God's prophet, confront thousands of people with such an offensive message that his God was going to overthrow Nineveh . . . and expect them to believe?[6]

Adad Gate of Nineveh, partially reconstructed

Can you imagine what Jonah must have been thinking as he walked toward the gates of this massive city? He was only one man, but he had been sent from God with a message he was prepared to deliver.

To this day, centuries later, this is still God's method of bringing about reformation, revival, and an awakening in any land. He works through a teacher, a Bible study leader, an evangelist, a counselor, a mentor, or a pastor who simply, clearly, and faithfully proclaims the words of God.

Reformation comes when the people of God submit to the will of God and communicate to their world the word of God. Then God does what only He can do.

Is it really that surprising to observe what happens next? Jonah 3:5 records, **Then the people of Nineveh believed in God.** Think about that. They **believed in God.** It does not say they believed in *Jonah.* They may have been somewhat swept up by the legend of Jonah, but they were ultimately swept away by the warning of Jonah and swept into the mercy of Jonah's God.

Martin Luther, the great reformer, was once asked about his incredible contribution to the Reformation, when the church and many millions of lives were changed. He responded, "I simply taught, preached, and wrote God's Word . . . I did nothing; the Word did everything." "The word of God is living and active and sharper than any two-edged sword, and piercing as far as the division of soul and spirit, of both joints and marrow, and able to judge the thoughts and intentions of the heart" (Hebrews 4:12).

A man who was given a second chance had fulfilled his sacred charge. The reformation of Nineveh was now underway.

⁵Then the people of Nineveh believed in God; and they called a fast and put on sackcloth from the greatest to the least of them. ⁶When the word reached the king of Nineveh, he arose from his throne, laid aside his robe from him, covered himself with sackcloth and sat on the ashes. ⁷He issued a proclamation and it said, "In Nineveh by the decree of the king and his nobles: Do not let man, beast, herd, or flock taste a thing. Do not let them eat or drink water. ⁸But both man and beast must be covered with sackcloth; and let men call on God earnestly that each may turn from his wicked way and from the violence which is in his hands. ⁹Who knows, God may turn and relent and withdraw His burning anger so that we will not perish." ¹⁰When God saw their deeds, that they turned from their wicked way, then God relented concerning the calamity which He had declared He would bring upon them. And He did not do it.

–Jonah 3:5–10

CHAPTER SIX

SEE JONAH REAP

Jonah 3:5–10

A decade ago the *Wall Street Journal* featured a front-page article entitled, "Confession Makes a Comeback." The article opened with these words: "Sin never goes out of style, but confession is undergoing a revival." The article went on to catalog the growth of new methods and means for confessing one's sins. There are websites that allow anonymous visitors to confess their sins. Some even allow other guests to read all the details of prior confessions.

In Colorado Springs, people can confess their sins during a trip to a local mall, where Catholic friars have set up shop for customers who want to make a quick confession. People can shop, grab a caramel latte, pop in for a confession, and head home absolved for yet another day.

The article went on to mention that just a year prior, the second-largest North American branch of the Lutheran Church (the Missouri Synod) voted to revive private confession with a priest.[1]

I did a little research and found additional creative ways for people to confess their sins, especially if they are embarrassed to admit anything in person. For a fee, one company allows people to talk on the telephone to one of their personnel and confess whatever plagues them.

Another company offers to go to a priest on behalf of its clients. In fact, the company will even apologize on their behalf, for a modest fee, of course.

Our world is filled with people struggling with guilt and an awareness of sin, and they are desperate to rid themselves of it.

I read about one man who went to his psychiatrist and said, "I've been doing a lot of bad things and my conscience is bothering me." The psychiatrist asked, "So you want something to strengthen your willpower?" The man said, "No, I want something to weaken my conscience."

True confession cannot be done online or on the telephone. And we cannot hire somebody to do it for us. True confession is directly admitting our sin to Jesus Christ, not to some earthly priest, because Christ is now High Priest and the only mediator between God and man (1 Timothy 2:5).

To avoid the Lord is to avoid genuine confession, and to avoid genuine confession is to miss genuine forgiveness, since Jesus Christ is the source of genuine forgiveness and cleansing from sin.

The Apostle Paul wrote to the Ephesians,

> In [Christ] we have redemption through His blood, the forgiveness of our trespasses, according to the riches of His grace which He lavished on us. (Ephesians 1:7–8)

If we want to see a biblical example of true confession; if we would like to see hearts exposed, sin admitted, and consequences accepted; we can find it in an unlikely place—in the city of Nineveh.

THE CITY'S REPENTANCE

In the English language, Jonah's sermon was only eight words long. He probably said more, but these eight words represent what we would identify as Jonah's main point: **"Yet forty days and Nineveh will be overthrown"** (Jonah 3:4*b*).

Now we can be certain Jonah spent some time telling the people about the true and living God, because we are told in the very next verse,

Then the people of Nineveh believed in God. (Jonah 3:5)

The Ninevites would have to know something about the God of Israel in order to transfer their faith from Dagon and other gods to Yahweh, the true and living God of heaven.[2]

The Hebrew word translated **believed** comes from a verb that means to *confirm* or to *support*. The tense of the verb indicates that the people considered everything Jonah said to be true.[3] Jonah delivered a very simple message, but it led the people to faith **in God**, *not* in Jonah. This was truly saving faith.

Charles Haddon Spurgeon, one of the most effective preachers in the English-speaking world, was saved by such a simple message. He was a young man at the time and had gone to a Primitive Methodist chapel to hear a sermon. When he arrived late, he discovered the pastor was not there. Actually, no one knew where the pastor was, and so after some awkward silence, one of the laymen stood to preach. Spurgeon later recounted the event in detail.

> He was obliged to stick to his text, for the simple reason that he had little else to say. The text was, "Look unto Me, and be ye saved." . . . The preacher began thus: "My dear friends," he said, "this is a very simple text indeed. It says, 'Look.' Now lookin' don't take a deal of pain. It ain't liftin' your foot or your finger; it is just, 'Look.' Well, a man needn't go to college to learn to look. You may be the biggest fool, and yet you can look. A man needn't be worth a thousand a year to be able to look. Anyone can look; even a child can look. But then the text says, 'Look unto Me.' . . . Many of you are lookin' to yourselves, but it's no use lookin' there. You'll never find any comfort in yourselves . . . Look to Christ. The text says, 'Look unto Me.'"[4]

After about ten minutes of such preaching, this layman had quite exhausted what he had to say. But when he noticed young Spurgeon sitting in the back under the balcony, not recognizing him and noticing his downcast expression, he called out to him,

> "Young man, you look miserable. . . . and you always will be miserable—miserable in life, and miserable in death—if you don't obey my text; but if you obey now, this moment, you will be saved. . . . Young man, look to Jesus Christ! Look! Look! Look!"[5]

With that, the sermon was finished. Yet God's clear invitation, delivered in such a simple manner, penetrated Spurgeon's heart. At that moment he looked to Christ alone and was indeed saved and his life changed.

With a similar and direct message, Jonah invited the Ninevites to look to the God of Israel. They did and were saved from God's judgment.

The proof of true confession is repentance, an about-face. Repentance means to turn around and head in the other direction. In fact, the New Testament word for repentance, metanoia (μετάνοια), literally means *a change of mind.*[6]

So, did these cruel, barbaric, arrogant, idolatrous people really change their minds and reveal a genuine belief in the God of Abraham, Isaac, and Jacob? As the events unfold, we are given two proofs of the genuineness of the Ninevites' confession.

1. **Their confession radically altered their personal priorities.**

    Then the people of Nineveh believed in God; and they called a fast and put on sackcloth from the greatest to the least of them. When the word reached the king of Nineveh, he arose from his throne, laid aside his robe from him, covered himself with sackcloth and sat on the ashes. (Jonah 3:5–6)

All the people, from king to commoner, exchanged their normal clothing for sackcloth. Sackcloth was a coarse, rough, dark-colored cloth usually made of goat hair, or cotton. It was used for making sacks for grain—think of a burlap bag. Whenever it was used for clothing, it represented humiliation and mourning.[7]

The king also **covered himself with sackcloth and sat on the ashes,** signifying his personal grief and humility.

Jonah 3:8 informs us they even covered their beasts with sackcloth. This was not because they believed their animals had sinned or that they could somehow repent, but so that even they would become an expression of humility and sorrow and grief.

Along with the wearing of sackcloth, we are told the people also **called a fast** (Jonah 3:5). The king later officially issued a proclamation that ordered a national fast (Jonah 3:7). They were going without food in order to dedicate their time to pray to God for His mercy.

We might be tempted to think, "Who wouldn't respond this way when they have been warned of judgment in forty days or less? Their only reason for following God must have been selfishness; they simply wanted to avoid His judgment."

I've met many unbelievers who know this verse by heart:

> For God so loved the world, that he gave his only begotten
> Son, that whosoever believeth in him should not perish, but
> have everlasting life. (John 3:16 KJV)

In other words, God loves you and sent His Son to die for you; and
if you believe in Him, you will not die and go to hell, but you will go to
heaven. This is essentially the gospel of Christ, and it includes the incentive
of avoiding judgment.

Even the context of John 3:16 is a conversation between Jesus and an
unbeliever named Nicodemus. This man had come to Jesus during the night
to ask how he could get into the kingdom of heaven. Jesus did not respond
by saying, "You're just being selfish!"

Later, the apostle Paul ended his sermon before the elite in Athens by
warning them, "God is now declaring to men that all people everywhere
should repent, because He has fixed a day in which He will judge the world"
(Acts 17:30–31). Here is a similar incentive to believe—to avoid the coming
judgment of God.

By the grace of God, the Ninevites believed the word of God and placed
their faith in God. And, yes, they were certainly motivated to do so by their
desire to avoid the judgment of God.

There is something else in this text that proves their confession was
genuine and much more than just self-seeking.

2. Their confession radically altered their public behavior.

> [The king] issued a proclamation and it said, "In Nineveh
> by the decree of the king and his nobles: Do not let man,
> beast, herd, or flock taste a thing. Do not let them eat or
> drink water. But both man and beast must be covered with
> sackcloth; and let men call on God earnestly that each may
> turn from his wicked way and from the violence which is
> in his hands. (Jonah 3:7–8)

The first proof of genuine confession was personal. This second proof
was public: There was a radical change in their public lifestyle.

Notice that the king did not bother proving to the people that they were wicked. He simply announced that all the people needed to turn from their wicked ways and from the violence for which they were known around the world. In other words, he was saying, "We all need to repent. We all need to turn around. We all need to change our minds and change our lives!"

Imagine this brutal warlord making such an announcement.

When I was in London some time ago, I had the opportunity to visit a site that had recently been opened for public touring. The city had opened the underground offices and sleeping quarters of Prime Minister Winston Churchill and his chiefs of staff during World War II.

This was the underground bunker, deep beneath the streets of London, where Churchill and his cabinet monitored the war efforts and ensured their survival while Hitler's Luftwaffe attempted to bomb England into submission.

Everything in the underground headquarters remained as it was when the war ended, left undisturbed for some sixty years. Chalkboards still had details written on them; maps opened on conference tables still showed troop locations; even a candy wrapper was still sitting near a typewriter. I was able to hear recordings of telephone conversations between Churchill and President Roosevelt.

Several times during the dark days of World War II, the king of England, as well as the president of the United States called for national days of prayer. Entire nations were encouraged to pray to the God of heaven. It is wonderful that such leaders would call upon their people to humbly pray to God. But I have never heard of any modern king or president calling for a national day of repentance.

It is one thing to call for people to pray; in fact, it is still politically acceptable during times of calamity, crisis, or even a drought. But it is another thing entirely to call for the people of one's nation to repent of their sins.

This Ninevite king was not merely calling for national prayer; he was calling for national repentance and personal purity. He was effectively announcing, "We're not going to rationalize our sin. We're not going to defend our violent acts on the basis that everybody else acts this way too. We're not going to excuse or minimize our sin or cover it up; we're going to admit it, confess it, and *stop it.*"

I must say I don't get excited when I hear some political and cultural figures call for prayer. Something bad happens, and suddenly, from political officials to news anchors, people are now "in our prayers." All that does is make unbelievers feel good and somewhat spiritual for a few days, and then it's back to living like their old selves again.

This was not the case in Nineveh. The people's confession was genuine, and this was evidenced by repentance that affected both personal priorities and public lifestyles.

GOD'S MERCY

Notice the open and honest hearts of the Ninevites, as expressed by their king:

> **"Who knows, God may turn and relent and withdraw His burning anger so that we will not perish."** (Jonah 3:9)

And note how God responded:

> **When God saw their deeds, that they turned from their wicked way, then God relented concerning the calamity which He had declared He would bring upon them. And He did not do it.** (Jonah 3:10)

From the human perspective, it appears that God changed His mind. But from the divine perspective, God was simply responding according to His purpose and promises to those who repent and confess their sins.

IMPORTANT LESSONS

If we learn anything from this amazing response of the Ninevites, it is to remember that God's mercy and grace can come to the most unlikely of people.

I doubt any faithful Jew living in Samaria or Jerusalem had the Ninevites on his or her prayer list. The Ninevites would never make the list of "most likely to believe."

Yet sometimes God's grace breaks through in unexpected ways and in unanticipated places. Who would ever have believed the people of Nineveh would repent and believe in God?

This is the point. If the Ninevites could repent, no one is too wicked to be excluded from our prayer list. No one is too violent, cruel, rebellious, immoral, or idolatrous that Christ cannot redeem that person.

Evan Roberts was a preacher God used to bring about an amazing awakening in Wales in the early 1900s.

It all began at a meeting with young people in his home. He challenged them to adopt four practices that would change their lives as believers:

1. Confess all known sin.

2. Stop any doubtful activities.

3. Be ready to obey the Holy Spirit's prompting immediately.

4. Publically confess Jesus Christ as Lord and Savior.

By the end of the first week, sixty young believers took up the challenge and began practicing these four distinctives. They confessed to Christ any secret or public sin. They stopped all doubtful or compromising activities, thus raising the standard of holy living. They began living with anticipation, sensitive to whatever God's Spirit prompted them to do, and this changed their work ethic, their relationships, and their character. Finally, whenever they had the chance, they told people they belonged to Jesus Christ.

The results were stunning. By the end of the second week, Evan Roberts began a whirlwind tour of South Wales with a team of musicians. Within one year, 100,000 people were genuinely converted to Jesus Christ and added to the church.

A description of the Welsh Revival reveals how lives were changed:

> As people confessed their sin and pleaded for the controlling of the Spirit of God, they did all they could to confess wrong doings and to make restitution [another proof of genuine repentance]. This unexpectedly created severe problems for the shipyards along the coast of Wales. Over the years workers had pilfered all kinds of things. Everything from wheelbarrows to hammers had been stolen. However, as people sought to be right with God, they started to return what they had taken, with the result that soon the shipyards of Wales were overwhelmed with returned property. There were such huge piles of returned tools that several of the yards actually put up

signs asking the men to stop. One sign read, "If you have been led by God to return what you have stolen, please know that the management forgives you and wishes you to keep what you had taken."[8]

What a change of heart. What a radical, public demonstration of repentance. And the world did not know how to handle such an awakening in people's lives.

A new—and needed—reformation will always follow this pattern. It begins with the commitment to preaching the message of God, followed by the commitment of people to confess all known sin, raise the standard of holy living beyond any doubtful activity, stay alert and obey whatever God's Spirit desires and prompts, and confess Christ in their public sphere of influence.

According to God's good pleasure, this may result in another national awakening. But if it does not, we can be sure it will bring about a fresh revival and awakening in our own hearts and lives.

We know from biblical history that Nineveh enjoyed a generation of walking with God. This was not a one-week revival. It was genuine. It took root.

Sadly, most of the descendants of the Ninevites in Jonah's day would return to idolatry, and around one hundred years after this great awakening, in 612 BC, God would indeed destroy Nineveh in judgment, as prophesied by Nahum.

However, this generation and their children, from king to commoner, believed, confessed, repented, and followed God. Imagine, we will one day meet converted Ninevites in heaven.

I have found it interesting that Assyrian Christians—that is, people from this region who trace their roots to ancient Nineveh—to this day "point to their faith as inspired by God's compassion toward Nineveh in sending Jonah to them and accepting their repentance."[9]

The Ninevites were lost in sin, hopeless and helpless before the coming judgment of God, but they believed the message of God and repented, and their lives were changed by the grace of God. If you likewise have believed in God and been changed by His grace, don't stop there.

- Continue confessing all known sin.

- Keep avoiding doubtful things that muddy your mind and dilute your testimony.

- Stay obedient to the Holy Spirit—open to His work and His will no matter how difficult or mundane.

- Commit to making your relationship with Jesus Christ public, speaking on His behalf as He gives you opportunities.

The work in Nineveh was not yet finished. In fact, there was one person who still needed a personal reformation—the prophet Jonah.

While the Ninevites had opened their hearts to God, Jonah had closed his. So our gracious God, who used Jonah's words, will—once again—begin to deal with Jonah's heart.

¹But it greatly displeased Jonah and he became angry. ²He prayed to the Lord and said, "Please Lord, was not this what I said while I was still in my own country? Therefore in order to forestall this I fled to Tarshish, for I knew that You are a gracious and compassionate God, slow to anger and abundant in lovingkindness, and one who relents concerning calamity. ³Therefore now, O Lord, please take my life from me, for death is better to me than life." ⁴The Lord said, "Do you have good reason to be angry?" ⁵Then Jonah went out from the city and sat east of it. There he made a shelter for himself and sat under it in the shade until he could see what would happen in the city. ⁶So the Lord God appointed a plant and it grew up over Jonah to be a shade over his head to deliver him from his discomfort. And Jonah was extremely happy about the plant. ⁷But God appointed a worm when dawn came the next day and it attacked the plant and it withered. ⁸When the sun came up God appointed a scorching east wind, and the sun beat down on Jonah's head so that he became faint and begged with all his soul to die, saying, "Death is better to me than life." ⁹Then God said to Jonah, "Do you have good reason to be angry about the plant?" And he said, "I have good reason to be angry, even to death." ¹⁰Then the Lord said, "You had compassion on the plant for which you did not work and which you did not cause to grow, which came up overnight and perished overnight. ¹¹Should I not have compassion on Nineveh, the great city in which there are more than 120,000 persons who do not know the difference between their right and left hand, as well as many animals?"

–Jonah 4:1–11

CHAPTER 7

SEE JONAH POUT

Jonah 4:1–11

I am convinced Jonah would have preferred that his little book ended with chapter 3. In fact, had the narrative ended at the conclusion of chapter 3, Jonah would have gone down in history, revered to this day, as the greatest evangelist-prophet who ever lived.

After five weeks of preaching, an entire city had repented and followed after God. And this was not just any city. This was Nineveh, the center of the cruel, idolatrous Assyrian Empire, known throughout the ancient world for its wickedness and brutality.

Jonah's world would have been shocked by the news of this great awakening in the east. Were Jonah alive today, his evangelistic crusade would be front-page news. He would be sought out for advice on every religious subject. Evangelists and pastors everywhere would be downloading his sermon outlines. Jonah would even be interviewed by the secular media curious to know what he had done to change an entire culture.

I can imagine mini-revivals springing up all around the world, following the methods of Jonah's forty-day walk through Nineveh. Banners would be flying outside circus tents promising "Revival Like Nineveh—Here This Week."

Authors would beg for Jonah's endorsement on books with titles like, *Effective Sermons for Effective Revivals* and *Redeeming A Nation in Forty Days or Less.*

No doubt Jonah would begin a bus tour instructing churches and Christian leaders on how to plant churches in former pagan temples.

Indeed, if Jonah were alive today, there would be invitations to appear on television and radio to describe life inside a whale, and featured articles would detail his closed-door meetings with the king of Nineveh and state dinners with the power brokers of Assyria. *Time Magazine* would elect him Person of the Year, and he would be awarded the Nobel Peace Prize for negotiating a lasting treaty with a brutal nation. Major streets would be renamed "Jonah Boulevard," and buses would deliver tourists to Jonah's hometown of Gath-hepher, where miniature whales would be on sale with little plastic men emerging from their mouths. Shops would be selling bathing suits with Jonah's picture on them.

I can even imagine at least two memorial parks in Joppa would be competing for tourists with their bigger-than-life statues of Jonah, one with a bronze plaque inscribed, "Jonah Started Out Here," and the other with a plague inscribed, "Jonah Spit Up Here." There would even be a little dent in the ground to mark the spot where he landed. Christian bookstores would have life-sized cardboard cutouts of Jonah so people could have their pictures taken standing beside God's greatest, most effective, most humble servant.

Think of the possibilities!

Fortunately, none of this could happen because, unfortunately for Jonah, his career did not end with chapter 3. As far as Jonah is concerned, this little book has one chapter too many.

Actually, it is just like God to record the rest of the story—that part of the story that would protect Jonah from becoming a celebrity for centuries to come. God's complete account keeps Jonah safely in the category of a clay pot God used in spite of himself, so that we glory, not in Jonah, but in Jonah's God.

The church in every generation is far too quick to make superstars out of saints. The result is that we have too many celebrities and not enough humble servants.

I believe this final chapter is the most critical one of all. Here we find the Lord asking His servant three penetrating questions—questions we all need to answer for ourselves. The first question concerns *perspective*, the second *priorities*, and the third *passion*.

JONAH'S MISDIRECTED PERSPECTIVE

Let's begin with the last verse of Jonah 3.

> **When God saw their deeds, that they turned from their wicked way, then God relented concerning the calamity which He had declared He would bring upon them. And He did not do it.** (Jonah 3:10)

Immediately following this at the beginning of chapter 4, we read:

> **But it greatly displeased Jonah and he became angry.** (Jonah 4:1)

If you have never read this account before, Jonah's reaction will come as a disappointing surprise.

Can you imagine someone preaching a forty-day evangelistic campaign in which everyone is converted, and the preacher goes home angry with the results? Of course not! You would expect Jonah to break out in praise to God for all the lost who had been redeemed and rescued from judgment.

What might be confusing at first, however, is actually explained by Jonah himself:

> **He prayed to the Lord and said, "Please, Lord, was not this what I said while I was still in my own country? Therefore in order to forestall this I fled to Tarshish, for I knew that You are a gracious and compassionate God, slow to anger and abundant in lovingkindness, and one who relents concerning calamity."** (Jonah 4:2)

Jonah had run from Nineveh in the first place, not because he was afraid no one would listen, but because he was afraid everyone *would*. He hated the Ninevites as much as they hated Israel. They were the enemy of his people, and the result of his preaching was the very thing Jonah had feared. He did not want them to be spared God's judgment.

Jonah was a super patriot—a defender of Israel and of the common belief that Israel had sole ownership of Yahweh.[1]

I agree with Warren Wiersbe, who stated:

> [Jonah's] Jewish friends would want to see all of the Assyrians destroyed, not just the people of Nineveh. When Jonah's friends found out that he had been the means of warning Nineveh of God's wrath, they could have considered him a traitor to official Jewish foreign policy.[2]

No wonder Jonah prayed,

"Therefore now, O Lord, please take my life from me, for death is better to me than life." (Jonah 4:3)

Jonah had prayed his best prayer in the worst place, the fish's belly, and he prayed his worst prayer in the best place, at Nineveh where God was working. His first prayer came from a broken heart, but his second prayer came from an angry heart.[3]

So God suddenly asked Jonah a question that we are allowed to hear:

The Lord said, "Do you have good reason to be angry?" (Jonah 4:4)

This question focused on perspective. God effectively was saying, "Jonah, we're looking at the same awakening. I am glad and the hosts of heaven are rejoicing, while you're growing angrier by the minute."

Jesus Christ looked at the city of Jerusalem and wept over the unbelief of the people (Luke 19:41). Paul walked around the city of Athens, where historians say the streets were filled with more statues of gods than people, and he was filled with alarm for their lost souls (Acts 17:16). Unfortunately, Jonah looked at the city of Nineveh and was angered that God had shown the people mercy.

God and Jonah had two very different perspectives; the Lord was basically asking Jonah which perspective was more reasonable.

You might have noticed the wonderful theology Jonah rehearsed in verse 2. He acknowledged the Lord as a **gracious and compassionate God, slow to anger and abundant in lovingkindness, and one who relents concerning calamity.**

This wonderful and accurate theology did not alter Jonah's perspective however. And it certainly did not affect his emotions. Jonah did not want truth to control his life.[4]

He could quote the truth; he just did not want to live it.

Can you imagine people coming to faith in Christ in your presence, and you mutter under your breath, "I was hoping they would die in their sins!" That is exactly how Jonah responded. In fact, his actions show that he was still hoping the repentance of the people was superficial.

> **Then Jonah went out from the city and sat east of it. There he made a shelter for himself and sat under it in the shade until he could see what would happen in the city.** (Jonah 4:5)

Were there no places for Jonah to stay in the city of Nineveh? Of course there were. The king's own palace would have been a wonderful retreat.[5]

Jonah, however, did not hang around Ninevites—even converted ones. They were not his kind of people. But there is more to this than national or personal prejudice. There is also the element of self-protection.

Jonah wanted to be far enough from the city that when the fire of God's judgment fell—as he hoped it would—it would not scorch *him*.

The word Jonah used to warn the Ninevites of being **overthrown** (Jonah 3:4) is the same word the Bible uses for Sodom and Gomorrah being overthrown by God (Genesis 19:25, 29). Jonah wanted to be at a safe distance from the fireworks.

Jonah was *hoping* the sky would light up with God's judgment; in fact, he was *counting* on it. Jonah wanted nothing more than for this Ninevite revival to turn into a national relapse. He was hoping the Ninevites would return to their idolatry so that on the forty-first day God's judgment would fall and reduce the city to a pile of smoldering ashes.

> **So the Lord God appointed a plant and it grew up over Jonah to be a shade over his head to deliver him from his discomfort. And Jonah was extremely happy about the plant.** (Jonah 4:6)

This is the first time in this whole narrative that Jonah is described as pleased. Jonah moved from anger in verse 1 to happiness in verse 6.

> **But God appointed a worm when dawn came the next day and it attacked the plant and it withered.** (Jonah 4:7)

The word for **worm** here refers to a fruit grub, which gnaws on the roots of vines and plants. It attacked this particular plant under divine orders.

We cannot help but notice that God **appointed** a great fish, a plant, and now a **worm**, and they *all* obeyed His command.

Everything in this book obeyed God except Jonah. Everything responded to God's command—the waves, the great fish, the plant, and now the worm. And let's not forget the Ninevites.

Now another obedient participant appears, right on cue from its Creator who **appointed** it.

> **When the sun came up God appointed a scorching east wind. And the sun beat down on Jonah's head so that he became faint [i.e., he fainted away and revived] and begged with all his soul to die, saying, "Death is better to me than life."** (Jonah 4:8)

This east wind was a *sirocco*, which is a hot dust storm that often lasts for days at a time. It created intense discomfort to Jonah, who again expressed his preference for death over life.

JONAH'S MISTAKEN PRIORITY

> **Then God said to Jonah, "Do you have good reason to be angry about the plant?" And he said, "I have good reason to be angry, even to death."** (Jonah 4:9)

God's first question exposed Jonah's misdirected perspective. This second question, in response to Jonah's plea to die, exposed a mistaken priority.

A good test question for revealing our priorities is this: What do I get excited about, and what do I get angry about? Or, in other words, what *turns* my engine and what *churns* my engine?

Jonah's current difficulty was the result of his own selfish anger. He could have been in the palace, away from the sun, protected from the dust storm, and sipping Assyrian sweet tea, but no, not Jonah. He wanted to see the Ninevites wiped from the face of the earth.

Jonah may have preached the message of God that led to spiritual awakening, but Jonah himself was obviously in need of a similar awakening. He was angry over the conversion of sinners and happy about the creation of a plant and then angry when the plant withered.[6] The prophet's distorted priority was fully exposed.

What makes us happy and what makes us angry reveal more about our priorities than we would often like to know. It's easy to say, "I can't believe Jonah became more upset over the condition of a plant than the condition of people."

Is that really so hard to believe? After all, it appears many people care more about their lawns than they do lost neighbors, at least based on how much time they spend gardening compared to evangelizing.

What do we *really* care about? What are our *real* priorities?

Recently, I heard an interview with a *Washington Post* reporter who said it seemed obvious from polls that even those who say they do not believe in terminating a preborn baby's life still vote for candidates who support abortion. Why? "Because," this man summarized, "even those who care about abortion evidently do not care about it as much as they do about their own personal finances."

Jonah cared more about his own personal comfort than he did the eternal condition of the Ninevites. He would fit nicely into many churches in this twenty-first century.

JONAH'S MISGUIDED PASSION

Then the Lord said, "You had compassion on the plant for which you did not work and which you did not cause to grow, which came up overnight and perished overnight. Should I not have compassion on Nineveh, the great city in which there are more than 120,000 persons who do not know the difference between their right and left hand, as well as many animals? (Jonah 4:10–11)

God's third and final question struck at Jonah's misguided passion. The Lord bluntly asked, **Should I not have compassion on Nineveh?** In other words, "Should I not be moved to pity and mercy? Should I not be moved on their behalf?"

Jonah had become passionate about the wrong thing. He was concerned about the *perishable* but not the *permanent.*

Everything on this planet is in the process of perishing. Only those things in the spiritual realm, including the existence of people's souls, will endure. This is where our priority should be.[7]

Notice what God pointed out to Jonah about Nineveh. He said there were 120,000 people in the city who did not know their right hand from their left. Some Bible scholars believe this is a reference to children who had not yet learned the difference between their right and left hands. Thus, God was pointing out Jonah's lack of compassion for the lives of 120,000 children.

It seems more likely God was referring to the citizens who lived within Nineveh's city walls, without counting the outlying suburbs, where perhaps another 500,000 people lived. In describing them as not knowing the difference **between their right and left hand,** God was reminding Jonah of how utterly confused and blinded they were because of their idolatry.

Throughout scripture, the **left hand** is a reference to ruin or spiritual blindness. Jesus Christ said that He will set His sheep on His right hand but the goats (unbelievers) will be placed at His left hand (Matthew 25:33).

On the other hand—literally—the right hand refers to spiritual power, fellowship, and righteousness. Jesus Christ ascended to the right hand of God the Father (Mark 16:19). Galatians 2:9 speaks of "the right hand of fellowship." And in Psalm 73:23 David rejoiced, saying, "I am continually with You; You have taken hold of my right hand."

God was more than likely reminding Jonah that the Ninevites had twisted all moral guidelines. Without true spiritual guidance, they had confused right for wrong and wrong for right.

Solomon wrote in Ecclesiastes 10:2, "A wise man's heart directs him toward the right, but the foolish man's heart directs him toward the left." Imagine, centuries ago, we find the metaphor of people belonging to the "right" and people belonging to the "left."

When people ask me for advice on who to vote for in upcoming elections, I often remind them of this verse: The wise move to the right and the fool moves to the left. Enough said.

God asked, "Jonah, **should I not have compassion** on all these morally misguided, spiritually blind people?" And with that question, the narrative ends. We are not even given Jonah's answer.

I would like to think he gave the right answer. I would like to think he packed up his gear and headed back to Nineveh to do some discipleship training.

There seems to be some evidence this, in fact, is exactly what happened. For centuries the area around Mosul has been known as Jonah's Hill. Furthermore, as mentioned earlier, Assyrian Christians still connect their salvation to the arrival of Jonah and his preaching of the gospel to their forefathers.

CONCLUSION

As we conclude our study of Jonah, we must note that Jonah's experiences point to One who is greater than Jonah.

Jesus used the three days Jonah was in the fish as an illustration of the three days and nights He Himself would be in the grave (Matthew 12:40). And just as Jonah effectively came back from the dead, so Jesus would rise from the grave.

In addition, our Lord said this:

> The men of Nineveh will stand up with this generation at the judgment, and will condemn it because they repented at the preaching of Jonah; and behold, [One] greater than Jonah is here. (Matthew 12:41)

The Ninevites repented at the preaching of Jonah, but Jerusalem did not repent at the preaching of Jesus, who was far *greater* than Jonah. Consider just a few of the ways in which Jesus was greater than Jonah:

- Jonah was a man; Jesus is the God-man (John 1).
- Jonah preached a message of judgment; Christ preached a message of repentance and salvation (John 3).
- Jonah almost died for his sins; Jesus died for the sins of the world (1 John 2).
- Jonah's obedience was partial; Jesus' obedience was total (John 8).

- Jonah did not love the people he addressed; Jesus had compassion for the lost and came to seek and to save them (Luke 19).

- Jonah waited outside the city, hoping God would not forgive his enemies; Christ was put on a cross outside the city, praying His Father would forgive His enemies (Luke 23).[8]

Jesus Christ is greater than Jonah in a million more ways.

This made the guilt of the Jews who rejected Jesus and His message all the greater. Even the pagan Ninevites had repented at the message delivered by God's weak and reluctant prophet.

And with that, the little book of Jonah ends as abruptly as it began. It ends with a question—in fact, several questions. Those divine questions focus on perspectives, priorities, and passions, and they are profound.

We cannot answer for Jonah, but we can answer for ourselves. Let's give God the right answers; let's obey Him like the wind and the waves and the fish and the worm and the plant . . . and the Ninevites. Let's refuse to hang a "Do Not Disturb" sign on the door of our hearts.

As we leave this journal of a prodigal prophet, it is clear the hero of the story is not Jonah. There's no need for Jonah's autograph or photograph. The hero is our gracious, long-suffering God.

To Him belong praise and honor and glory forever and ever!

ENDNOTES

CHAPTER ONE

1   James Bruckner, *NIV Application Bible: Jonah, Nahum, Habakkuk, Zephaniah* (Zondervan, 2004), 17.

2   Thomas L. Constable, *Online Notes on Jonah: 2008 Edition.* http://www.soniclight.com, 1.

3   These objections are discussed in James Montgomery Boice, *The Minor Prophets, Volume 1* (Baker, 1983), 262.

4   Henry M. Morris, *The Remarkable Journey of Jonah* (Master Books, 2003), 18.

5   J. Sidlow Baxter, *Explore the Book* (Zondervan, 1960), 148.

6   Ibid., 19.

7   Quoted in T. Desmond Alexander, "Jonah," in David W. Baker, T. Desmond Alexander, and Bruce K. Watlke, *Obadiah, Jonah, Micah* (InterVarsity Press, 1988), 75.

8   Warren W. Wiersbe, *Be Amazed* (Victor Books, 2004), 71.

9   Bruckner, 41.

10   Joyce Baldwin, "Jonah," in *The Minor Prophets: An Exegetical and Expository Commentary,* ed. by Thomas E. McComiskey, Vol. 2 (Baker, 1993), 552.

11   William L. Banks, *Jonah: The Reluctant Prophet* (Moody Press, 1966), 13.

12   Ibid., 14.

13   Adapted from Warren W. Wiersbe, *Life Sentences: Key Themes of 63 Bible Characters* (Zondervan, 2007), 175.

14   John Phillips, *Exploring the Minor Prophets* (Kregel, 1998), 137.

CHAPTER TWO

1   See The Living Bible paraphrase.

2   T. Desmond Alexander, "Jonah," in David W. Baker, T. Desmond Alexander, and Bruce K. Watlke, *Obadiah, Jonah, Micah* (InterVarsity Press, 1988), 98.

3   Sadly, much of the reconstruction of the gates and walls of Nineveh were destroyed by ISIS jihadists in 2016.

4   H. W. F. Saggs, *The Babylonians* (London, 1962), p. 94.

5   James Bruckner, *NIV Application Bible: Jonah, Nahum, Habakkuk, Zephaniah* (Zondervan, 2004), 28.

6 William L. Banks, *Jonah: The Reluctant Prophet* (Moody Press, 1966), 14.

7 Sinclair B. Ferguson, *Man Overboard* (Banner of Truth Trust, 1981), 12.

8 David J. Clark, Norm Mundhenk, Eugene A. Nida, and Brynmor F. Price, *A Handbook on the Books of Obadiah, Jonah, and Micah* (United Bible Societies, 1993), 53.

9 James Montgomery Boice, *The Minor Prophets, Volume 1* (Baker Books, 1983), 266.

10 Quoted in John Phillips, *Exploring the Minor Prophets* (Kregel, 1998), 141.

11 Dan Schmidt, *Unexpected Wisdom* (Baker, 2002), 1.

12 Phillips, 142.

CHAPTER THREE

1 "Wanted Man Caught by Kiss Kam," Preachingtoday.com, from Associated Press, May 30, 2003.

2 Trent C. Butler, *Holman Old Testament Commentary: Hosea-Micah* (Holman Reference, 2005), 273.

3 David J. Clark, Norm Mundhenk, Eugene A. Nida, and Brynmor F. Price, *A Handbook on the Books of Obadiah, Jonah, and Micah* (United Bible Societies, 1993), 56.

4 William L. Banks, *Jonah: The Reluctant Prophet* (Moody Press, 1966), 24.

5 Ibid., 57.

6 John Phillips, *Exploring The Minor Prophets* (Kregel, 1998), 143.

7 Banks, 30.

8 "Driver Leads Cops on 15-Mile Chase," *Chicago Sun-Times,* December 2, 2004.

9 The translations here are from the Good News Translation and the New Living Translation respectively.

10 James Montgomery Boice, *The Minor Prophets, Volume 1* (Baker Books, 1983), 279.

CHAPTER FOUR

1 Cited by William L. Banks, *Jonah: The Reluctant Prophet* (Moody Press, 1966), 44.

2 Cited by David J. Clark, Norm Mundhenk, Eugene A. Nida, and Brynmor F. Price, *A Handbook on the Books of Obadiah, Jonah, and Micah* (United Bible Societies, 1993), 73.

3 James Montgomery Boice, *The Minor Prophets, Volume 1* (Baker Books, 1983), 282.

4 Boice, 284.

5 Warren W. Wiersbe, *Be Amazed* (Victor Books, 2004), 78.

6   Ibid.

7   Ibid., 79.

8   Sinclair B. Ferguson, *Man Overboard* (Banner of Truth Trust, 1981), 30.

9   Boice, 288.

10 Cited in Trent C. Butler, *Holman Old Testament Commentary: Hosea-Micah* (Holman Reference, 2005), 276.

CHAPTER FIVE

1   Walter C. Kaiser, *Toward an Exegetical Theology* (Baker, 1981), 7-8.

2   James Montgomery Boice, *The Minor Prophets, Volume 1* (Baker Books, 1983), 292.

3   William L. Banks, *Jonah: The Reluctant Prophet* (Moody Press, 1966), 72.

4   Quoted in Warren W. Wiersbe, *Be Amazed* (Victor Books, 2004), 83.

5   Ibid., 84.

6   Ibid., 85.

CHAPTER SIX

1   "Confession Makes a Comeback," *The Wall Street Journal* (September 21, 2007).

2   Warren W. Wiersbe, *Be Amazed* (Victor Books, 2004), 86.

3   William L. Banks, *Jonah: The Reluctant Prophet* (Moody Press, 1966), 85.

4   John Mulder, ed., *Finding God: A Treasury of Conversion Stories* (Eerdmans, 2012), 135.

5   Ibid., 136.

6   W. E. Vine, *Expository Dictionary of Old and New Testament Words* (Thomas Nelson, 1997), 952.

7   Banks, 88.

8   This familiar description is attributed to J. Edwin Orr, renowned authority on the history of revivals.

9   James Bruckner, *NIV Application Bible: Jonah, Nahum, Habakkuk, Zephaniah* (Zondervan, 2004), 102.

CHAPTER SEVEN

1   William L. Banks, *Jonah: The Reluctant Prophet* (Moody Press, 1966), 105.

2   Warren W. Wiersbe, *Be Amazed* (Victor Books, 2004), 88.

3   Ibid., 89.

4   Howard Hendricks, "Jonah: The Pouting Prophet," 1. discipleshiplibrary.com.

[5]   James Montgomery Boice, *The Minor Prophets, Volume 1* (Baker Books, 1983), 308.

[6]   Hendricks, 2.

[7]   Hendricks, 3.

[8]   Wiersbe, 93.

PHOTO CREDITS

Page 9: Nineveh Map. By Fredarch. CC Attribution Share-Alike 3.0.

Page 19: Reconstructed Nirgal Gate at Nineveh (2008). Public Domain photo by U. S. Air Force.

Page 20: Depiction of interior of Nineveh Palace. Photo by Patrick Gray from Momuments of Nineveh. CC Attribution 2.0 Generic.

Page 21: Assyrian king putting out the eyes of captive, who, with others, is held prisoner with hooks in the lips. Public domain. Image from *A Comprehensive Dictionary of the Bible* (1871) by William Smith.

Page 24: Port city of Jaffa, biblical Joppa. By StateofIsrael. CC ShareAlike Generic 2.0.

Page 25: Map by Jarl K. Waggoner.

Page 59: Winged bulls. British Museum. ChameleonsEye / Shutterstock Inc.

Page 60: Fish-god Dagon. Public domain. *A Dictionary of Universal Knowledge for the People* (1881) by William and Robert Chambers.

Page 61: Partially reconstructed Adad Gate of Nineveh. Photo by Fredarch. CC attribution-Share Alike 3.0.

SCRIPTURE INDEX